EURIPID

ALCESTIS

MEDEA

THE CHILDREN OF HERACLES

HIPPOLYTUS

THE COMPLETE GREEK TRAGEDIES

Edited by David Grene & Richmond Lattimore

THIRD EDITION *Edited by Mark Griffith & Glenn W. Most*

EURIPIDES I

ALCESTIS *Translated by Richmond Lattimore*

MEDEA *Translated by Oliver Taplin*

THE CHILDREN OF HERACLES *Translated by Mark Griffith*

HIPPOLYTUS *Translated by David Grene*

The University of Chicago Press CHICAGO & LONDON

MARK GRIFFITH is professor of classics and of theater, dance, and performance studies at the University of California, Berkeley.

GLENN W. MOST is professor of ancient Greek at the Scuola Normale Superiore at Pisa and a visiting member of the Committee on Social Thought at the University of Chicago.

DAVID GRENE (1913–2002) taught classics for many years at the University of Chicago.

RICHMOND LATTIMORE (1906–1984), professor of Greek at Bryn Mawr College, was a poet and translator best known for his translations of the Greek classics, especially his versions of the *Iliad* and *Odyssey*.

The University of Chicago Press, Chicago 60637
The University of Chicago Press, Ltd., London
© 2013 by The University of Chicago

Hippolytus © 1942, 2013 by the University of Chicago
Alcestis © 1955, 2013 by the University of Chicago
Medea and *The Children of Heracles* © 2013 by the University of Chicago

27 26 25 24 23 22   10

ISBN-13: 978-0-226-30879-1 (cloth)
ISBN-13: 978-0-226-30880-7 (paper)
ISBN-13: 978-0-226-30934-7 (e-book)
ISBN-10: 0-226-30879-0 (cloth)
ISBN-10: 0-226-30880-4 (paper)
ISBN-10: 0-226-30934-7 (e-book)

Library of Congress Cataloging-in-Publication Data
Euripides.
 [Works. English. 2012]
 Euripides. — Third edition.
 volumes cm. — (The complete Greek tragedies)
 ISBN 978-0-226-30879-1 (v. 1 : cloth : alk. paper) — ISBN 0-226-30879-0 (v. 1 : cloth : alk. paper) — ISBN 978-0-226-30880-7 (v. 1 : pbk. : alk. paper) — ISBN 0-226-30880-4 (v. 1 : alk. paper) — ISBN 978-0-226-30934-7 (v. 1 : e-book) — ISBN 0-226-30934-7 (v. 1 : e-book) — ISBN 978-0-226-30877-7 (v. 2 : cloth : alk. paper) — ISBN 0-226-30877-4 (v. 2 : cloth : alk. paper) — ISBN 978-0-226-30878-4 (v. 2 : pbk. : alk. paper) — ISBN-10: 0-226-30878-2 (v. 2 : pbk. : alk. paper) —ISBN 978-0-226-30935-4 (v. 2 : e-book) — ISBN-10: 0-226-30935-5 (v. 2 : e-book) —ISBN 978-0-226-30881-4 (v. 3 : cloth : alk. paper) — ISBN 0-226-30881-2 (v. 3 : cloth : alk. paper) — ISBN 978-0-226-30882-1 (v. 3 : pbk. : alk. paper) — ISBN 0-226-30882-0 (v. 3 : pbk. : alk. paper) — ISBN 978-0-226-30936-1 (v. 3 : e-book) — ISBN 0-226-30936-3 (v. 3 : e-book)
 1. Euripides—Translations into English. 2. Mythology, Greek—Drama. I. Lattimore, Richmond Alexander, 1906–1984. II. Taplin, Oliver. III. Griffith, Mark, Ph. D. IV. Grene, David. V. Roberts, Deborah H. VI. Arrowsmith, William, 1924–1992. VII. Jones, Frank William Oliver, 1915– VIII. Vermeule, Emily. IX. Carson, Anne, 1950– X. Willetts, R. F. (Ronald Frederick), 1915–1999. XI. Euripides. Alcestis. English. XII. Title. XIII. Series: Complete Greek tragedies (Unnumbered)
 PA3975.A1 2012
 882'.01—dc23

                                    2012015831

♾ This paper meets the requirements of ANSI/NISO Z39.48-1992 (Permanence of Paper).

CONTENTS

EDITORS' PREFACE TO THE THIRD EDITION

The first edition of the *Complete Greek Tragedies*, edited by David Grene and Richmond Lattimore, was published by the University of Chicago Press starting in 1953. But the origins of the series go back even further. David Grene had already published his translation of three of the tragedies with the same press in 1942, and some of the other translations that eventually formed part of the Chicago series had appeared even earlier. A second edition of the series, with new translations of several plays and other changes, was published in 1991. For well over six decades, these translations have proved to be extraordinarily popular and resilient, thanks to their combination of accuracy, poetic immediacy, and clarity of presentation. They have guided hundreds of thousands of teachers, students, and other readers toward a reliable understanding of the surviving masterpieces of the three great Athenian tragedians: Aeschylus, Sophocles, and Euripides.

But the world changes, perhaps never more rapidly than in the past half century, and whatever outlasts the day of its appearance must eventually come to terms with circumstances very different from those that prevailed at its inception. During this same period, scholarly understanding of Greek tragedy has undergone significant development, and there have been marked changes not only in the readers to whom this series is addressed, but also in the ways in which these texts are taught and studied in universities. These changes have prompted the University of Chicago Press to perform another, more systematic revision of the translations, and we are honored to have been entrusted with this delicate and important task.

Our aim in this third edition has been to preserve and strengthen as far as possible all those features that have made the Chicago translations successful for such a long time, while at the same time revising the texts carefully and tactfully to bring them up to date and equipping them with various kinds of subsidiary help, so they may continue to serve new generations of readers.

Our revisions have addressed the following issues:

- Wherever possible, we have kept the existing translations. But we have revised them where we found this to be necessary in order to bring them closer to the ancient Greek of the original texts or to replace an English idiom that has by now become antiquated or obscure. At the same time we have done our utmost to respect the original translator's individual style and meter.
- In a few cases, we have decided to substitute entirely new translations for the ones that were published in earlier editions of the series. Euripides' *Medea* has been newly translated by Oliver Taplin, *The Children of Heracles* by Mark Griffith, *Andromache* by Deborah Roberts, and *Iphigenia among the Taurians* by Anne Carson. We have also, in the case of Aeschylus, added translations and brief discussions of the fragments of lost plays that originally belonged to connected tetralogies along with the surviving tragedies, since awareness of these other lost plays is often crucial to the interpretation of the surviving ones. And in the case of Sophocles, we have included a translation of the substantial fragmentary remains of one of his satyr-dramas, *The Trackers* (*Ichneutai*). (See "How the Plays Were Originally Staged" below for explanation of "tetralogy," "satyr-drama," and other terms.)
- We have altered the distribution of the plays among the various volumes in order to reflect the chronological order in which they were written, when this is known or can be estimated with some probability. Thus the *Oresteia* appears now as volume 2 of Aeschylus' tragedies, and the sequence of Euripides' plays has been rearranged.
- We have rewritten the stage directions to make them more consistent throughout, keeping in mind current scholarly under-

standing of how Greek tragedies were staged in the fifth century BCE. In general, we have refrained from extensive stage directions of an interpretive kind, since these are necessarily speculative and modern scholars often disagree greatly about them. The Greek manuscripts themselves contain no stage directions at all.

• We have indicated certain fundamental differences in the meters and modes of delivery of all the verse of these plays. Spoken language (a kind of heightened ordinary speech, usually in the iambic trimeter rhythm) in which the characters of tragedy regularly engage in dialogue and monologue is printed in ordinary Roman font; the sung verse of choral and individual lyric odes (using a large variety of different meters), and the chanted verse recited by the chorus or individual characters (always using the anapestic meter), are rendered in *italics*, with parentheses added where necessary to indicate whether the passage is sung or chanted. In this way, readers will be able to tell at a glance how the playwright intended a given passage to be delivered in the theater, and how these shifting dynamics of poetic register contribute to the overall dramatic effect.

• All the Greek tragedies that survive alternate scenes of action or dialogue, in which individual actors speak all the lines, with formal songs performed by the chorus. Occasionally individual characters sing formal songs too, or they and the chorus may alternate lyrics and spoken verse within the same scene. Most of the formal songs are structured as a series of pairs of stanzas of which the metrical form of the first one ("strophe") is repeated exactly by a second one ("antistrophe"). Thus the metrical structure will be, e.g., strophe A, antistrophe A, strophe B, antistrophe B, with each pair of stanzas consisting of a different sequence of rhythms. Occasionally a short stanza in a different metrical form ("mesode") is inserted in the middle between one strophe and the corresponding antistrophe, and sometimes the end of the whole series is marked with a single stanza in a different metrical form ("epode")—thus, e.g., strophe A, mesode, antistrophe A; or strophe A, antistrophe A, strophe B, antistrophe B, epode. We have indicated these metrical structures by inserting the terms

STROPHE, ANTISTROPHE, MESODE, and EPODE above the first line of the relevant stanzas so that readers can easily recognize the compositional structure of these songs.

- In each play we have indicated by the symbol ° those lines or words for which there are significant uncertainties regarding the transmitted text, and we have explained as simply as possible in textual notes at the end of the volume just what the nature and degree of those uncertainties are. These notes are not at all intended to provide anything like a full scholarly apparatus of textual variants, but instead to make readers aware of places where the text transmitted by the manuscripts may not exactly reflect the poet's own words, or where the interpretation of those words is seriously in doubt.
- For each play we have provided a brief introduction that gives essential information about the first production of the tragedy, the mythical or historical background of its plot, and its reception in antiquity and thereafter.
- For each of the three great tragedians we have provided an introduction to his life and work. It is reproduced at the beginning of each volume containing his tragedies.
- We have also provided at the end of each volume a glossary explaining the names of all persons and geographical features that are mentioned in any of the plays in that volume.

It is our hope that our work will help ensure that these translations continue to delight, to move, to astonish, to disturb, and to instruct many new readers in coming generations.

MARK GRIFFITH, *Berkeley*
GLENN W. MOST, *Florence*

INTRODUCTION TO EURIPIDES

Little is known about the life of Euripides. He was probably born between 485 and 480 BCE on the island of Salamis near Athens. Of the three great writers of Athenian tragedy of the fifth century he was thus the youngest: Aeschylus was older by about forty years, Sophocles by ten or fifteen. Euripides is not reported to have ever engaged significantly in the political or military life of his city, unlike Aeschylus, who fought against the Persians at Marathon, and Sophocles, who was made a general during the Peloponnesian War. In 408 Euripides left Athens to go to the court of King Archelaus of Macedonia in Pella (we do not know exactly why). He died there in 406.

Ancient scholars knew of about ninety plays attributed to Euripides, and he was given permission to participate in the annual tragedy competition at the festival of Dionysus on twenty-two occasions—strong evidence of popular interest in his work. But he was not particularly successful at winning the first prize. Although he began competing in 455 (the year after Aeschylus died), he did not win first place until 441, and during his lifetime he received that award only four times; a fifth victory was bestowed on him posthumously for his trilogy *Iphigenia in Aulis*, *The Bacchae*, *Alcmaeon in Corinth* (this last play is lost), produced by one of his sons who was also named Euripides. By contrast, Aeschylus won thirteen victories and Sophocles eighteen. From various references, especially the frequent parodies of Euripides in the comedies of Aristophanes, we can surmise that many members of contemporary Athenian audiences objected to Euripides' tendency to make the characters of tragedy more modern and less heroic, to represent the passions of women, and to reflect recent developments in philosophy and music.

But in the centuries after his death, Euripides went on to become by far the most popular of the Greek tragedians. When the ancient Greeks use the phrase "the poet" without further specification and do not mean by it Homer, they always mean Euripides. Hundreds of fragments from his plays, mostly quite short, are found in quotations by other authors and in anthologies from the period between the third century BCE and the fourth century CE. Many more fragments of his plays have been preserved on papyrus starting in the fourth century BCE than of those by Aeschylus and Sophocles together, and far more scenes of his plays have been associated with images on ancient pottery starting in the same century and on frescoes in Pompeii and elsewhere and Roman sarcophagi some centuries later than is the case for either of his rivals. Some knowledge of his texts spread far and wide through collections of sententious aphorisms and excerpts of speeches and songs drawn from his plays (or invented in his name).

It was above all in the schools that Euripides became the most important author of tragedies: children throughout the Greek-speaking world learned the rules of language and comportment by studying first and foremost Homer and Euripides. But we know that Euripides' plays also continued to be performed in theaters for centuries, and the transmitted texts of some of the more popular ones (e.g., *Medea, Orestes*) seem to bear the traces of modifications by ancient producers and actors. Both in his specific plays and plots and in his general conception of dramatic action and character, Euripides massively influenced later Greek playwrights, not only tragic poets but also comic ones (especially Menander, the most important dramatist of New Comedy, born about a century and a half after Euripides)—and not only Greek ones, but Latin ones as well, such as Accius and Pacuvius, and later Seneca (who went on to exert a deep influence on Renaissance drama).

A more or less complete collection of his plays was made in Alexandria during the third century BCE. Whereas, out of all the plays of Aeschylus and Sophocles, only seven tragedies each were chosen (no one knows by whom) at some point later in antiquity, probably in the second century CE, to represent their work, Euripides received the distinction of having ten plays selected as canonical: *Alcestis, Andromache, The Bacchae, Hecuba, Hippolytus, Medea, Orestes, The Phoenician Women, Rhesus* (scholars generally think this play was written by someone other than Euripides and was attributed to him in antiquity by mistake), and *The Trojan Women*. Of these ten tragedies, three—*Hecuba, Orestes,* and *The Phoenician Women*—were especially popular in the Middle Ages; they are referred to as the Byzantine triad, after the capital of the eastern Empire, Byzantium, known later as Constantinople and today as Istanbul.

The plays that did not form part of the selection gradually ceased to be copied, and thus most of them eventually were lost to posterity. We would possess only these ten plays and fragments of the others were it not for the lucky chance that a single volume of an ancient complete edition of Euripides' plays, arranged alphabetically, managed to survive into the Middle Ages. Thus we also have another nine tragedies (referred to as the alphabetic plays) whose titles in Greek all begin with the letters *epsilon, êta, iota,* and *kappa: Electra, Helen, The Children of Heracles (Hêrakleidai), Heracles, The Suppliants (Hiketides), Ion, Iphigenia in Aulis, Iphigenia among the Taurians,* and *The Cyclops (Kyklôps).* The Byzantine triad have very full ancient commentaries (scholia) and are transmitted by hundreds of medieval manuscripts; the other seven plays of the canonical selection have much sparser scholia and are transmitted by something more than a dozen manuscripts; the alphabetic plays have no scholia at all and are transmitted only by a single manuscript in rather poor condition and by its copies.

Modern scholars have been able to establish a fairly secure dating for most of Euripides' tragedies thanks to the exact indications provided by ancient scholarship for the first production of some of them and the relative chronology suggested by metrical and other features for the others. Accordingly the five volumes of this third edition have been organized according to the probable chronological sequence:

Volume 1: *Alcestis*: 438 BCE
           Medea: 431
           The Children of Heracles: ca. 430
           Hippolytus: 428
Volume 2: *Andromache*: ca. 425
           Hecuba: ca. 424
           The Suppliant Women: ca. 423
           Electra: ca. 420
Volume 3: *Heracles*: ca. 415
           The Trojan Women: 415
           Iphigenia among the Taurians: ca. 414
           Ion: ca. 413
Volume 4: *Helen*: 412
           The Phoenician Women: ca. 409
           Orestes: 408
Volume 5: *The Bacchae*: posthumously after 406
           Iphigenia in Aulis: posthumously after 406
           The Cyclops: date unknown
           Rhesus: probably spurious, from the fourth century BCE

In the Renaissance Euripides remained the most popular of the three tragedians. Directly and by the mediation of Seneca he influenced drama from the sixteenth to the eighteenth century far more than Aeschylus or Sophocles did. But toward the end of the eighteenth century and even more in the course of the nineteenth century, he came increasingly under attack yet again, as already in the fifth century BCE, and for much the same reason, as being decadent, tawdry, irreligious, and inharmonious. He was also criticized for his perceived departures from the ideal of "the tragic" (as exemplified by plays such as Sophocles' *Oedipus the*

King and *Antigone*), especially in the "romance" plots of *Alcestis*, *Iphigenia among the Taurians*, *Ion*, and *Helen*. It was left to the twentieth century to discover its own somewhat disturbing affinity to his tragic style and worldview. Nowadays among theatrical audiences, scholars, and nonprofessional readers Euripides is once again at least as popular as his two rivals.

HOW THE PLAYS WERE ORIGINALLY STAGED

Nearly all the plays composed by Aeschylus, Sophocles, and Euripides were first performed in the Theater of Dionysus at Athens, as part of the annual festival and competition in drama. This was not only a literary and musical event, but also an important religious and political ceremony for the Athenian community. Each year three tragedians were selected to compete, with each of them presenting four plays per day, a "tetralogy" of three tragedies and one satyr-play. The satyr-play was a type of drama similar to tragedy in being based on heroic myth and employing many of the same stylistic features, but distinguished by having a chorus of half-human, half-horse followers of Dionysus—sileni or satyrs—and by always ending happily. Extant examples of this genre are Euripides' *The Cyclops* (in *Euripides*, vol. 5) and Sophocles' *The Trackers* (partially preserved: in *Sophocles*, vol. 2).

The three competing tragedians were ranked by a panel of citizens functioning as amateur judges, and the winner received an honorific prize. Records of these competitions were maintained, allowing Aristotle and others later to compile lists of the dates when each of Aeschylus', Sophocles', and Euripides' plays were first performed and whether they placed first, second, or third in the competition (unfortunately we no longer possess the complete lists).

The tragedians competed on equal terms: each had at his disposal three actors (only two in Aeschylus' and in Euripides' earliest plays) who would often have to switch between roles as each play progressed, plus other nonspeaking actors to play attendants and other subsidiary characters; a chorus of twelve (in Aeschylus' time) or fifteen (for most of the careers of Sophocles and Euripides), who would sing and dance formal songs and whose Chorus Leader would engage in dialogue with the characters or offer comment on the action; and a pipe-player, to accompany the sung portions of the play.

All the performers were men, and the actors and chorus members all wore masks. The association of masks with other Dionysian rituals may have affected their use in the theater; but masks had certain practical advantages as well—for example, making it easy to play female characters and to change quickly between roles. In general, the use of masks also meant that ancient acting techniques must have been rather different from what we are used to seeing in the modern theater. Acting in a mask requires a more frontal and presentational style of performance toward the audience than is usual with unmasked, "realistic" acting; a masked actor must communicate far more by voice and stylized bodily gesture than by facial expression, and the gradual development of a character in the course of a play could hardly be indicated by changes in his or her mask. Unfortunately, however, we know almost nothing about the acting techniques of the Athenian theater. But we do know that the chorus members were all Athenian amateurs, and so were the actors up until the later part of the fifth century, by which point a prize for the best actor had been instituted in the tragic competition, and the art of acting (which of course included solo singing and dancing) was becoming increasingly professionalized.

The tragedian himself not only wrote the words for his play but also composed the music and choreography and directed the productions. It was said that Aeschylus also acted in his plays but that Sophocles chose not to, except early in his career, because his voice was too weak. Euripides is reported to have had a collaborator who specialized in musical composition. The costs for each playwright's production were shared between an individual wealthy citizen, as a kind of "super-tax" requirement, and the city.

The Theater of Dionysus itself during most of the fifth century BCE probably consisted of a large rectangular or trapezoidal dance floor, backed by a one-story wooden building (the *skênê*), with a large central door that opened onto the dance floor. (Some scholars have argued that two doors were used, but the evidence is thin.) Between the *skênê* and the dance floor there may have been a narrow stage on which the characters acted and which communicated easily with the dance floor. For any particular play, the *skênê* might represent a palace, a house, a temple, or a cave, for example; the interior of this "building" was generally invisible to the audience, with all the action staged in front of it. Sophocles is said to have been the first to use painted scenery; this must have been fairly simple and easy to remove, as every play had a different setting. Playwrights did not include stage directions in their texts. Instead, a play's setting was indicated explicitly by the speaking characters.

All the plays were performed in the open air and in daylight. Spectators sat on wooden seats in rows, probably arranged in rectangular blocks along the curving slope of the Acropolis. (The stone semicircular remains of the Theater of Dionysus that are visible today in Athens belong to a later era.) Seating capacity seems to have been four to six thousand—thus a mass audience, but not quite on the scale of the theaters that came to be built during the fourth century BCE and later at Epidaurus, Ephesus, and many other locations all over the Mediterranean.

Alongside the *skênê*, on each side, there were passages through which actors could enter and exit. The acting area included the dance floor, the doorway, and the area immediately in front of the *skênê*. Occasionally an actor appeared on the roof or above it, as if flying. He was actually hanging from a crane (*mêchanê*: hence *deus ex machina*, "a god from the machine"). The *skênê* was also occasionally opened up—the mechanical details are uncertain—in order to show the audience what was concealed within (usually dead bodies). Announcements of entrances and exits, like the setting, were made by the characters. Although the medieval manuscripts of the surviving plays do not provide explicit stage directions, it is usually possible to infer from the words or from the context whether a particular entrance or exit is being made through a door (into the *skênê*) or by one of the side entrances. In later antiquity, there may have been a rule that one side entrance always led to the city center, the other to the countryside or harbor. Whether such a rule was ever observed in the fifth century is uncertain.

ALCESTIS

Translated by RICHMOND LATTIMORE

ALCESTIS: INTRODUCTION

The Play: Date and Composition

Euripides' *Alcestis* was produced in 438 BCE at the Great Dionysian Festival in Athens as one of four plays in a tetralogy of which
the other three plays have been lost: *The Cretan Women*, *Alcmaeon
in Psophis*, and *Telephus*. Euripides took the second prize that year
behind Sophocles. Although *Alcestis* is Euripides' earliest securely
dated play, he was probably in his forties at the time and had been
competing in the dramatic contests for over fifteen years (though
he had not won his first victory until 441).

Ancient scholars reported that *Alcestis* was performed fourth
in Euripides' tetralogy that year and thus took the place of the
satyr-play, the comic play centered on Dionysus and his troop of
ribald satyrs that usually followed the three serious and lofty tragedies in any entry in the dramatic competition. Ancient scholars also pointed out the elements of the play that reminded them
more of comedy or of satyr-plays than of tragedy—above all, the
fact that events turn out happily in the end. They even suggested
that *Alcestis* was not to be considered a genuine tragedy. Modern
scholars have continued to debate this question. Just what kind
of play is *Alcestis*? To which genre or genres, if any, should it be
assigned?

The Myth

Alcestis tells how the god Apollo tries to reward Admetus, king of
the town of Pherae in Thessaly, for his hospitality to him by ar-
ranging that a substitute die in the king's stead on the fated day
of his death. Admetus' parents refuse to sacrifice their lives for

him, but his wife, Alcestis, agrees to do so. After she dies, Admetus' friend Heracles shows up; Admetus conceals the news of Alcestis' death and receives him with great hospitality. When Heracles discovers what has happened, he wrestles with Death, defeats him, and leads Alcestis back to Admetus.

The story of the man doomed to die who seeks, and sometimes finds, a substitute willing to die in his place is a widespread motif of folktales from many places and ages. Familiar too from folktales, though less widely attested, is the idea that a hero can wrestle with Death and rescue someone from his clutches. But there are few if any traces of such topics in surviving Greek literature before Euripides. The only important predecessor about whom we have any information is the Greek tragedian Phrynichus, active at the end of the sixth century and the beginning of the fifth century BCE: an *Alcestis* is listed among his works, and the few fragments and references to this lost play that can be gleaned from later authors indicate that it probably included some of the same characters who appear in Euripides' version (especially Apollo, Death, and Heracles) and that Phrynichus may have been the one who invented the fundamental idea of Alcestis being rescued from the dead. Although the main characters of Euripides' play were certainly familiar to his audience, at least as names, it is likely that the specific plot Euripides constructed for them was surprising and fresh.

Transmission and Reception

After Euripides, comic and tragic dramas about Alcestis were occasionally produced by other Greek and Roman authors; at Rome, Alcestis was also a subject for pantomimes. About these later dramatic versions we know too little to be able to say how much Euripides' play influenced them. So too, there are only occasional references to the story of Alcestis among ancient poets and prose writers, who did sometimes mention her briefly as a celebrated example of a loyal wife but generally did not pause to consider in any depth her psychology or her husband's. But there are at least two remarkable instances of the influence of the *Alcestis* in late antiquity: a Latin poem entitled *Alcesta*, which narrates the myth in 162 verses, all recycled entirely from the works of Virgil; and a papyrus of the fourth century CE, recently discovered in Barcelona, which bears 122 lines of a semidramatic poem in Latin about the story of Alcestis and Admetus, demonstrating some knowledge of Euripides' play.

The play survived as a text in the schools and for some private readers, and it belongs to the group of ten plays by Euripides that were most widely diffused during ancient and medieval times. More even than in literature, Alcestis enjoyed remarkable popularity in ancient pictorial art. She appears especially on Roman sarcophagi, presumably as an exemplar of conjugal fidelity and of hopes for the afterlife. Unsurprisingly, the scene that is most often depicted is that of Heracles leading her back from the dead.

In modern times *Alcestis* has never been among Euripides' most popular plays and has not often been staged. But it has provided the inspiration for various successful dramatic and operatic versions, including operas by Philippe Quinault (1674), George Frideric Handel (1727), and especially Christoph Willibald Gluck (1767), and plays by Christoph Martin Wieland (1773; satirized by Johann Wolfgang von Goethe in the same year), Vittorio Alfieri (1806), and Hugo von Hofmannsthal. The Victorian poet Robert Browning interpreted the story of Alcestis in his *Balaustion's Adventure* (1871); other notable lyric versions include those by Rainer Maria Rilke (1904), Erica Jong (ca. 1973), and Donald Justice (1979). In the theater, more or less radical transformation of the Euripidean model has inspired such very different plays as T. S. Eliot's *The Cocktail Party* (1949), Thornton Wilder's *The Alcestiad; or, A Life in the Sun* (1955), Efua Sutherland's Ghanan *Edufa* (ca. 1962), and Marguerite Yourcenar's *Le mystère d'Alceste* (1963), as well as Martha Graham's dance drama *Alcestis* (1960). It has also been depicted in several modern paintings (Jacques-Louis David, 1767; Eugène Delacroix, 1851–52, 1862) and sculptures (Auguste Rodin, 1899).

ALCESTIS

Scene: *Pherae, in Thessaly, in front of the house of Admetus*

> *(Enter Apollo from the house, armed with a bow.)*

APOLLO

House of Admetus, in which I, god though I am,
had patience to accept the table of the serfs!
Zeus was the cause. Zeus killed my son, Asclepius,
and drove the bolt of the hot lightning through his chest.
I, in my anger for this, killed the Cyclopes,   5
smiths of Zeus's fire, for which my father made me serve
a mortal man, in penance for what I did.
I came to this country, tended the oxen of this host
and friend, Admetus, son of Pheres, and have kept
his house from danger until this very day.   10
For I, who know what's right, have found in him
a man who knows what's right, and so I saved him

from dying, tricking the Fates. The goddesses promised me
Admetus would escape the moment of his death
by giving the lower powers someone else to die
instead of him. He tried his loved ones all in turn,   15
father and aged mother who had given him birth,°
and found not one, except his wife, who would consent
to die for him, and not see daylight any more.
She is in the house now, gathered in his arms and held
at the breaking point of life, because destiny marks   20
this for her day of death and taking leave of life.
The stain of death in the house must not be on me. I
step therefore from these chambers dearest to my love.
And here is Death himself, I see him coming, Death
who dedicates the dying, who will lead her down   25
to the house of Hades. He has come on time. He has
been watching for this day on which her death falls due.

(Enter Death from the side, armed with a sword.)

DEATH [chanting]
  Ah!
  You at this house, Phoebus? Why do you haunt
  the place? It is unfair to take for your own   30
  and spoil the death-spirits' privileges.
  Was it not enough, then, that you blocked the death
  of Admetus, and overthrew the Fates
  by a shabby wrestler's trick? And now
  your bow hand is armed to guard her too,   35
  Alcestis, Pelias' daughter, though she
  promised her life for her husband's.

APOLLO
  Never fear. I have nothing but justice and fair words for you.

DEATH [now speaking]
  If you mean fairly, what are you doing with a bow?

APOLLO
  It is my custom to carry it with me all the time.   40

DEATH

It is your custom to help this house more than you ought.

APOLLO

But he is my friend, and his misfortunes trouble me.

DEATH

You mean to take her corpse, too, away from me?

APOLLO

I never took his body away from you by force.

DEATH

How is it, then, that he is above ground, not below?   45

APOLLO

He gave his wife instead, and you have come for her now.

DEATH

I have. And I shall take her down where the dead are.

APOLLO

Take her and go. I am not sure you will listen to me.

DEATH

Tell me to kill whom I must kill. Such are my orders.

APOLLO

No, only to put their death off. They must die in the end.   50

DEATH

I understand what you would say and what you want.

APOLLO

Is there any way, then, for Alcestis to grow old?

DEATH

There is not. I insist on enjoying my rights too.

APOLLO

You would not take more than one life, in any case.

DEATH

My privilege means more to me when they die young.   55

APOLLO

If she dies old, she will have a lavish burial.

DEATH

What you propose, Phoebus, is to favor the rich.

APOLLO

What is this? Have you unrecognized talents for debate?

DEATH

Those who could afford to buy a late death would buy it then.

APOLLO

I see. Are you determined not to do this favor for me?   60

DEATH

I will not do it. And you know my character.

APOLLO

I know it: hateful to mankind, loathed by the gods.

DEATH

You cannot always have your way where you should not.

APOLLO

For all your brute ferocity you shall be stopped.
The man to do it is on the way to Pheres' house   65
now, on an errand from Eurystheus, sent to steal
a team of horses from the wintry lands of Thrace.
He shall be entertained here in Admetus' house
and he shall take the woman away from you by force,
nor will you have our gratitude, but you shall still   70
be forced to do it, and to have my hate beside.

DEATH

Much talk. Talking will win you nothing. All the same,
the woman will go with me to Hades' house. I go
to her now, to dedicate her with my sword,
for all whose hair is cut in consecration   75
by this blade's edge are devoted to the gods below.

(Exit Death into the house, Apollo to the side. Enter the Chorus.)

CHORUS° [*chanting*]
   It is quiet by the palace. What does it mean?
   Why is the house of Admetus so still?
   Is there none here of his family, none
   who can tell us whether the queen is dead   80
   and therefore to be mourned? Or does Pelias'
   daughter Alcestis live still, still look
   on daylight, she who in my mind appears
   noble beyond
   all women beside in a wife's duty?   85
   [*singing individually, not as a group*]

FIRST CITIZEN

STROPHE A
   Does someone hear anything?
   a groan or a hand's stroke or outcry
   in the house, as if something were done
   and over?

SECOND CITIZEN
              No. And there is no servant stationed
   at the outer gates. O Paean,   90
   healer, might you show in light
   to still the storm of disaster.

THIRD CITIZEN
   They would not be silent if she were dead.

FOURTH CITIZEN
   No, she is gone.°

FIFTH CITIZEN
   They have not taken her yet from the house.

SIXTH CITIZEN
   So sure? I know nothing. Why are you certain?   95
   And how could Admetus have buried his wife
   with none by, and she so splendid?

SEVENTH CITIZEN

ANTISTROPHE A

Here at the gates I do not see
the lustral spring water, approved
by custom for a house of death.   100

EIGHTH CITIZEN

Nor are there cut locks of hair at the forecourts
hanging, such as the stroke of sorrow
for the dead makes. I can hear no beating
of the hands of young women.

NINTH CITIZEN

Yet this is the day appointed.   105

TENTH CITIZEN

What do you mean? Speak.

NINTH CITIZEN

On which she must pass to the world below.

ELEVENTH CITIZEN

You touch me deep, my heart, my mind.

TWELFTH CITIZEN

Yes. He who from the first has claimed to be called
a good man himself   110
must grieve when good men are afflicted.

[all singing together]

STROPHE B

Sailing the long sea, there is
not any shrine on earth
you could visit, not Lycia,
not the unwatered sanctuary of Ammon,   115
to redeem the life
of this unhappy woman. Her fate shows
steep and near. There is no god's hearth
I know you could reach and by sacrifice   120
avail to save.

There was only one. If the eyes
of Phoebus' son Asclepius could have
seen this light, if he could have come
and left the dark chambers,   125
the gates of Hades.
He upraised those who were stricken
down, until from Zeus' hand
the flown bolt of thunder hit him.
Where is there any hope for life   130
left for me any longer?

[*now chanting*]
For all has been done that can be done by our kings now,
and there on all the gods' altars
are blood sacrifices dripping in full,
but no healing comes for the evil.   135

(Enter Maid from the house.)

CHORUS LEADER

But here is a serving woman coming from the house.
The tears break from her. What will she say has taken place?
We must, of course, forgive your sorrow if something
has happened to your masters. We should like to know
whether the queen is dead or if she is still alive.   140

MAID

I could tell you that she is still alive or that she is dead.

CHORUS LEADER

How could a person both be dead and live and see?

MAID

It has felled her, and the life is breaking from her now.

CHORUS LEADER

Such a husband, to lose such a wife! I pity you.

MAID

The master does not see it and he will not see it   145
until it happens.

CHORUS LEADER

There is no hope left she will live?

MAID

None. This is the day of destiny. It is too strong.

CHORUS LEADER

Surely, he must be doing all he can for her.

MAID

All is prepared so he can bury her in style.

CHORUS LEADER

Let her be sure, at least, that as she dies, there dies   150
the noblest woman underneath the sun, by far.

MAID

Noblest? Of course the noblest, who will argue that?
What shall the wife be who surpasses her? And how
could any woman show that she loves her husband more
than herself better than by consent to die for him?   155
But all the city knows that well. You shall be told
now how she acted in the house, and be amazed
to hear. For when she understood the appointed day
was come, she bathed her white body with water drawn
from running streams, then opened the cedar chest and took   160
her clothes out, and dressed in all her finery
and stood before the shrine of Hestia, and prayed:
"Mistress, since I am going down beneath the ground,
I kneel before you in this last of all my prayers.
Take good care of my children for me. Give the boy   165
a loving wife; give the girl a noble husband;
and do not let my children die like me, who gave
them birth, untimely. Let them live a happy life

through to the end and prosper here in their own land."
Afterward she approached the altars, all that stand 170
in the house of Admetus, made her prayers, and decked
    them all
with fresh sprays torn from living myrtle. And she wept
not at all, made no outcry. The advancing doom
made no change in the color and beauty of her face.
But then, in their room, she threw herself upon the bed, 175
and there she did cry, there she spoke: "O marriage bed,
it was here that I undressed my maidenhood and gave
myself up to this husband for whose sake I die.
Good-bye. I hold no grudge. But you have been my death
and mine alone. I could not break my faith with you and him: 180
I die. Some other woman will possess you now.
She will not be better, but she might be happier."
She fell on the bed and kissed it. All the coverings
were drenched in the unchecked outpouring of her tears;
but after much crying, when all her tears were shed, 185
she rolled from the couch and walked away with eyes cast
    down,
began to leave the room, but turned and turned again
to fling herself once more upon the bed. Meanwhile
the children clung upon their mother's dress, and cried,
until she gathered them into her arms, and kissed 190
first one and then the other, as in death's farewell.
And all the servants in the house were crying now
in sorrow for their mistress. Then she gave her hand
to each, and each one took it, there was none so mean
in station that she did not stop and talk with him. 195
This is what Admetus and the house are suffering. Had
he died, he would have lost her, but in this escape
he will keep such pain; it will not ever go away.

CHORUS LEADER
    Admetus surely must be grieving over this
    when such a wife must be taken away from him. 200

MAID

Oh yes, he is crying. He holds his wife close in his arms,
imploring her not to forsake him. What he wants
is impossible. She is dying. The sickness fades her now.
She has gone slack, just an inert weight on the arm.
Still, though so little breath of life is left in her, 205
she wants to look once more upon the light of the sun,
since this will be the last time of all, and never again.°
She must see the sun's shining circle yet one more time.
Now I must go announce your presence. It is not
everyone who bears so much good will toward our kings 210
as to stand by ready to help in their distress.
But you have been my master's friends since long ago.

(*Exit Maid into the house.*)

CHORUS° [*singing*]

STROPHE

O Zeus, Zeus, what way out of this evil
is there, what escape from this
which is happening to our princes?
A way, any way?° Must I cut short my hair 215
for grief, put upon me the black
costume that means mourning?
We must, friends, clearly we must; yet still
let us pray to the gods. The gods
have power beyond all power elsewhere.

Paean, my lord, 220
Apollo, make some way of escape for Admetus.
Grant it, oh grant it. Once you found
rescue in him. Be now
in turn his redeemer from death.
Oppose bloodthirsty Hades. 225

ANTISTROPHE

Admetus,
O son of Pheres, what a loss

to suffer, when such a wife goes.
A man could cut his throat for this, for this
and less he could bind the noose upon his neck
and hang himself. For this is   230
not only dear, but dearest of all,
this wife you will see dead
on this day before you.

> (Enter Alcestis carried from the house on a litter, supported
> by Admetus and followed by her children and servants.)

But see, see,
she is coming out of the house and her husband is with her.
Cry out aloud, mourn, you land
of Pherae for the bravest   235
of wives fading in sickness and doomed
to the Death God of the world below.

[now chanting]
I will never again say that marriage brings
more pleasure than pain. I judge by what
I have known in the past, and by seeing now   240
what happens to our king, who is losing a wife
brave beyond all others, and must live a life
that will be no life for the rest of time.

ALCESTIS [singing in the following interchange with Admetus, while he
speaks in reply]

STROPHE A

Sun, and light of the day,
O turning wheel of the sky, clouds that fly.   245

ADMETUS

The sun sees you and me, two people suffering,
who never hurt the gods so they should make you die.

ALCESTIS

ANTISTROPHE A

My land, and palace arching my land,
and marriage chambers of Iolcus, my own country.

ADMETUS

Raise yourself, my Alcestis, do not leave me now.   250
I implore the gods to pity you. They have the power.

ALCESTIS

STROPHE B

I see him there at the oars of his little boat in the lake,
the ferryman of the dead,
Charon, with his hand upon the oar,
and he calls me now: "What keeps you?   255
Hurry, you hold us back." He is urging me on
in angry impatience.

ADMETUS

The crossing you speak of is a bitter one for me;
ill starred; it is unfair we should be treated so.

ALCESTIS

ANTISTROPHE B

Somebody takes me, takes me, somebody takes me,
don't you see, to the courts   260
of dead men. He frowns from under dark
brows. He has wings. It is Hades.
Let me go, what are you doing, let go.
                                        Such is the road
most wretched I have to walk.

ADMETUS

Sorrow for all who love you, most of all for me
and for the children. All of us share in this grief.   265

ALCESTIS

EPODE

Let me go now, let me down,
flat. I have no strength to stand.
Hades is close to me.
The darkness creeps over my eyes. O children,
my children, you have no mother now,   270

not any longer. Daylight is yours, my children.
Look on it and be happy.

ADMETUS [*now chanting*]
Ah, a bitter word for me to hear,
heavier than any death for me.
Please by the gods, do not be so harsh   275
as to leave me, please, by your children forlorn.
No, up, and fight it.
There would be nothing left of me if you died.
All rests in you, our life, our not
having life. Your love is what we hold sacred.

ALCESTIS [*speaking*]
Admetus, you can see how it is with me. Therefore,   280
I wish to have some words with you before I die.
I put you first, and at the price of my own life
made certain you would live and see the daylight. So
I die, who did not have to die, because of you.
I could have taken any man in Thessaly   285
I wished and lived in queenly state here in this house.
But since I did not wish to live bereft of you
and with our children fatherless, I did not spare
my youth, although I had so much to live for. Yet
your father, and the mother who bore you, betrayed you,   290
though they had reached an age when it was good to die
and good to save their son and end it honorably.
You were their only one, and they had no more hope
of having other children if you died. That way
I would be living and you would live the rest of our time, 295
and you would not be alone and mourning for your wife
and tending motherless children. No, but it must be
that some god has so wrought that things shall be this way.
So be it. But swear now to do, in recompense,
what I shall ask you—not enough, oh, never enough,   300
since nothing is enough to make up for a life,
but fair, and you yourself will say so, since you love

these children as much as I do; or at least you should.
Keep them as masters in my house, and do not marry
again and give our children a stepmother   305
who will not be so kind as I, who will be jealous
and raise her hand to your children and mine. Oh no,
do not do that, do not. That is my charge to you.
For the new-come stepmother hates the children born
to a first wife; no viper could be deadlier.   310
The little boy has his father for a tower of strength.°
But you, my darling, what will your girlhood be like,
how will your father's new wife like you? She must not
make shameful stories up about you, and contrive   315
to spoil your chance of marriage in the blush of youth.
Indeed, your mother will not be there to help you
when you are married, not be there to give you strength
when your babies are born, when only a mother's help will do.
For I must die. It will not be tomorrow, not   320
the next day, or this month, the horrible thing will come,
but now, at once, I shall be counted among the dead.
Good-bye, be happy, both of you. And you, my husband,
can boast the bride you took made you the bravest wife,
and you, children, can say, too, that your mother was brave. 325

CHORUS LEADER
Fear nothing; for I dare to speak for him. He will
do all you ask. If he does not, it's his mistake.

ADMETUS
It shall be so, it shall be, do not fear, since you
were mine in life, you still shall be my bride in death
and you alone, no other girl in Thessaly   330
shall ever be called wife of Admetus in your place.
There is none so marked out in pride of father's birth
nor other form of beauty's brilliant gleam. I have
these children, they are enough; I only pray the gods
grant me the bliss to keep them as we could not keep you.   335
I shall go into mourning for you, not for just

a year, but all my life while it still lasts, my dear,
and hate the woman who gave me birth always, detest
my father. These were called my own dear ones. They were not.
You gave what was your own and dear to buy my life 340
and saved me. Am I not to lead a mourning life
when I have lost a wife like you? I shall make an end
of revelry and entertainment in my house,
the flowers and the music that here once held sway.
No, I shall never touch the lute strings ever again 345
nor have the heart to play music upon the pipe
of Libya, for you took my joy in life with you.
The skillful hands of craftsmen shall be set to work
making me an image of you to set in my room;
I'll pay my devotions to it, hold it in my arms 350
and speak your name, and clasp it close against my heart,
and think I hold my wife again, though I do not,
cold consolation, I know it, and yet even so
I might drain the weight of sorrow. You would come
to see me in my dreams and comfort me. For they 355
who love find a time's sweetness in the visions of night.
Had I the lips of Orpheus and his melody
to charm the maiden Daughter of Demeter and
her lord, and by my singing win you back from death,
I would have gone beneath the earth: not Pluto's hound 360
Cerberus could have stayed me, not the ferryman
of ghosts, Charon at his oar. I would have brought you back
to life. Wait for me, then, in that place, till I die,
and make ready the room where you will live with me,
for I shall have them bury me in the same chest 365
as you, and lay me at your side, so that my heart
shall be against your heart, and never, even in death
shall I go from you. You alone were true to me.

CHORUS LEADER
    And I, because I am your friend and you
    are mine, shall help you bear this sorrow, as I should. 370

ALCESTIS

Children, you now have heard your father promise me
that he will never marry again and not inflict
a new wife on you, but will honor my memory.

ADMETUS

I promise again. I will keep my promise to the end.

ALCESTIS

On this condition, take the children. They are yours.   375

ADMETUS

I take them, a dear gift from a dear hand.

ALCESTIS

                                        And now
you must be our children's mother, too, instead of me.

ADMETUS

I must be such, since they will no longer have you.

ALCESTIS

O children, this was my time to live, and I must go.

ADMETUS

Ah me, what shall I do without you all alone?   380

ALCESTIS

Time will soften this. The dead count for nothing at all.

ADMETUS

Oh, take me with you, for god's love, take me down there too.

ALCESTIS

No, I am dying in your place. That is enough.

ADMETUS

O god, what a wife you are taking away from me!

ALCESTIS

It is true. My eyes darken and the heaviness comes.   385

ADMETUS

But I am lost, dear, if you leave me.

ALCESTIS

There is no use
in talking to me any more. I am not there.

ADMETUS

No, lift your head up, do not leave your children thus.

ALCESTIS

I do not want to, but it is good-bye, children.

ADMETUS

Look at them—oh, look at them!

ALCESTIS

No. There is nothing more.   390

ADMETUS

Are you really leaving us?

ALCESTIS

Good-bye.

ADMETUS

Oh, I am lost.

CHORUS LEADER

It is over now. Admetus' wife is gone from us.

BOY° [*singing*]

STROPHE

O wicked fortune. Mother has gone down there,
father; she is not here with us
in the sunshine any more.   395
Poor mother, she went away
and left me to live all alone.
Look at her eyes, look at her hands, so still.
Hear me, mother, listen to me, oh please,   400

listen, it is I, mother,
I your little one lean and kiss
your lips, and cry out to you.

ADMETUS

She does not see, she does not hear you. You two and I
all have a hard and heavy load to carry now. 405

BOY

ANTISTROPHE

Father, I am too small to be left alone
by the mother I loved so much. Oh,
it is hard for me to bear
all this that is happening,
and you, little sister, suffer 410
with me too.° Oh, father,
your marriage was useless, useless; she did not live
to grow old with you.
She died too soon. Mother, with you gone away,
the whole house is ruined. 415

(Exit Alcestis carried into the house, followed by children and servants.)

CHORUS LEADER

Admetus, you must stand up to misfortune now.
You are not the first, and not the last of humankind
to lose a good wife. Therefore, you must understand
death is an obligation claimed from all of us.

ADMETUS

I understand it. And this evil which has struck 420
was no surprise. I knew about it long ago,
and knowledge was hard. But now, since we must bury our
    dead,
stay with me and stand by me, chant in response the hymn
to the god below who never receives libations.
To all Thessalians over whom my rule extends 425
I ordain a public mourning for my wife, to be

observed with shaving of the head and with black robes.
The horses that you drive in chariots and those
you ride single shall have their manes cut short with steel,
and there shall be no sound of pipes within the city,   430
no sound of lyres, until twelve moons have filled and gone;
for I shall never bury any dearer dead
than she, nor any who was better to me. She deserves
my thanks. She died for me, which no one else would do.

(Exit into the house.)

CHORUS [*singing*]

STROPHE A

O daughter of Pelias   435
my wish for you is a happy life
in the sunless chambers of Hades.
Now let the dark-haired lord of Death himself, and the old man,
who sits at the steering oar   440
and ferries the corpses,
know that you are the bravest of wives, by far,
ever conveyed across the lake
of Acheron in the rowboat.

ANTISTROPHE A

Much shall be sung of you   445
by the men of music to the seven-strung mountain
lyre-shell, and in poems that have no music,
in Sparta when the season turns and the month Carneian
comes back, and the moon
rides all the night;   450
in Athens also, the shining and rich.
Such is the theme of song you left
in death, for the poets.

STROPHE B

Oh, that it were in my power   455
and that I had strength to bring you
back to light from the dark of death°

with oars on the sunken river.
For you, O dearest among women, only you   460
had the hard courage
to give your life for your husband's and save
him from death. May the dust lie light
upon you, my lady. And should he now take
a new wife to his bed, he will win my horror and hatred,
mine, and your children's hatred too.   465

ANTISTROPHE B

His mother would not endure
to have her body hidden in the ground
for him, nor the aged father.°
He was theirs, but they had not courage to save him.
Oh shame, for the gray was upon them.   470
But you, in the pride
of youth, died for him and left the daylight.
May it only be mine to win
such wedded love as hers from a wife; for this
is given seldom to mortals; but were my wife such, I would have her
with me unhurt through my lifetime.   475

(Enter Heracles from the side.)

HERACLES

My friends, people of Pherae and the villages
hereby, tell me, shall I find Admetus at home?

CHORUS LEADER

Yes, Heracles, the son of Pheres is in the house.
But tell us, what is the errand that brings you here
to the land of Thessaly and this city of Pherae?   480

HERACLES

I have some work to do for Eurystheus
of Tiryns.

CHORUS LEADER

Where does it take you? On what far journey?

HERACLES

To Thrace, to take home Diomedes' chariot.

CHORUS LEADER

How can you? Do you know the man you are to meet?

HERACLES

No. I have never been where the Bistones live.   485

CHORUS LEADER

You cannot master his horses. Not without a fight.

HERACLES

It is my work, and I cannot refuse.

CHORUS LEADER

You must
kill him before you come back; or be killed and stay.

HERACLES

If I must fight, it will not be for the first time.

CHORUS LEADER

What good will it do you if you overpower their master?   490

HERACLES

I will take the horses home to Tiryns and its king.

CHORUS LEADER

It is not easy to put a bridle on their jaws.

HERACLES

Easy enough, unless their nostrils are snorting fire.

CHORUS LEADER

Not that, but they have teeth that tear a man apart.

HERACLES

Oh no! Mountain beasts, not horses, feed like that.   495

CHORUS LEADER

But you can see their mangers. They are caked with blood.

HERACLES

And the man who raises them? Whose son does he claim
to be?

CHORUS LEADER

Ares'. And he is lord of the golden shield of Thrace.

HERACLES

It sounds like my life and the kind of work I do.
It is a hard and steep way always that I go,   500
having to fight one after another all the sons
the war god ever got him, with Lycaon first,
again with Cycnus, and now here is a third fight
that I must have with the master of these horses. So—
I am Alcmene's son, and the man does not live   505
who will see me break before my enemy's attack.

CHORUS LEADER

Here is the monarch of our country coming
from the house himself, Admetus.

(Enter Admetus from the house.)

ADMETUS

                                        Welcome and happiness
to you, O scion of Perseus' blood and child of Zeus.

HERACLES

Happiness to you likewise, lord of Thessaly,   510
Admetus.

ADMETUS

                        I could wish it. I know you mean well.

HERACLES

What is the matter? Why is there mourning and cut hair?

ADMETUS

There is one dead here whom I must bury today.

HERACLES

Not one of your children! I pray some god shield them from
   that.

ADMETUS

Not they. My children are well and living in their house.   515

HERACLES

If it is your father who is gone, his time was ripe.

ADMETUS

No, he is still there, Heracles. My mother, too.

HERACLES

Surely you have not lost your wife, Alcestis.

ADMETUS

                                                         Yes
and no. There are two ways that I could answer that.

HERACLES

Did you say that she is dead or that she is still alive?   520

ADMETUS

She is, and she is no longer. It pains me.

HERACLES

I still do not know what you mean. You are being obscure.

ADMETUS

You know about her and what must happen, do you not?

HERACLES

I know that she has undertaken to die for you.

ADMETUS

How can she still be alive, then, when she has promised that?   525

HERACLES

Ah, do not mourn her before she dies. Wait for the time.

ADMETUS

The point of death is death, and the dead are lost and gone.

HERACLES

Being and nonbeing are considered different things.

ADMETUS

That is your opinion, Heracles. It is not mine.

HERACLES

Well, but whose is the mourning now? Is it in the family?   530

ADMETUS

A woman. We were speaking of a woman, were we not?

HERACLES

Was she a blood relative or someone from outside?

ADMETUS

No relation by blood, but she meant much to us.

HERACLES

How does it happen that she died here in your house?

ADMETUS

She lost her father and came here to live with us.   535

HERACLES

I am sorry,
Admetus. I wish I had found you in a happier state.

ADMETUS

Why do you say that? What do you mean to do?

HERACLES

                                        I mean
to go on, and stay with another of my friends.

ADMETUS

No, my lord, no. The evil must not come to that.

HERACLES

The friend who stays with friends in mourning is in the way. 540

ADMETUS

The dead are dead. Go on in.

HERACLES

No. It is always wrong
for guests to revel in a house where others mourn.

ADMETUS

There are separate guest chambers. We will take you there.

HERACLES

Let me go, and I will thank you a thousand times.

ADMETUS

You shall not go to stay with any other man. 545
You there: open the guest rooms which are across the court
from the house, and tell the people who are there to provide
plenty to eat, and make sure that you close the doors
facing the inside court. It is not right for guests
to have their pleasures interrupted by sounds of grief. 550

(Heracles is escorted into the house.)

CHORUS LEADER

Admetus, are you crazy? What are you thinking of
to entertain guests in a situation like this?

ADMETUS

And if I had driven from my city and my house
the guest and friend who came to me, would you have
approved
of me more? Wrong. My misery would still have been 555
as great, and I should be inhospitable too,
and there would be one more misfortune added to those
I have, if my house is called unfriendly to its friends.
For this man is my best friend, and he is my host
whenever I go to Argos, which is a thirsty place. 560

CHORUS LEADER

Yes, but then why did you hide what is happening here
if this visitor is, as you say, your best friend?

ADMETUS

He would not have been willing to come inside my house
if he had known what trouble I was in. I know.
There are some will think I show no sense in doing this.   565
They will not like it. But my house does not know how
to push its friends away and not treat them as it should.

(Exit into the house.)

CHORUS [*singing*]

STROPHE A

O liberal and forever free-handed house of this man,
the Pythian himself, lyric Apollo,   570
was pleased to live with you
and had patience upon your lands
to work as a shepherd,
and on the hill-folds and the slopes   575
piped to the pasturing of your flocks
in their season of mating.

ANTISTROPHE A

And even dappled lynxes for delight in his melody
joined him as shepherds. From the cleft of Othrys descended   580
a red troop of lions,
and there, Phoebus, to your lyre's strain
there danced the bright-coated
fawn, adventuring from the deep   585
bearded pines, light-footed for joy
in your song, in its kindness.

STROPHE B

Therefore, your house is beyond
all others for wealth of flocks by the sweet waters
of Lake Boebias. For spread of cornland   590

and pasturing range its boundary stands
only there where the sun
stalls his horses in dark air by the Molossians.
Eastward he sways all to the harborless 595
Pelian coast on the Aegean main.

Now he has spread wide his doors
and taken the guest in, when his eyes were wet
and he wept still for a beloved wife who died
in the house so lately. The noble strain 600
comes out, in respect for others.
All is there in the noble. I stand
in awe at his wisdom,° and good hope has come again to my heart
that for this godly man the end will be good. 605

(*Enter Admetus from the house, followed by*
servants with a covered litter.)

ADMETUS

Gentlemen of Pherae, I am grateful for your company.
My men are bearing to the burning place and grave
our dead, who now has all the state which is her due.
Will you then, as the custom is among us, say
farewell to the dead as she goes forth for the last time? 610

CHORUS LEADER

Yes, but I see your father coming now. He walks
as old men do, and followers carry in their hands
gifts for your wife, to adorn her in the underworld.

(*Enter Pheres from the side.*)

PHERES

I have come to bear your sorrows with you, son. I know,
nobody will dispute it, you have lost a wife 615
both good and modest in her ways. Nevertheless,
you have to bear it, even though it is hard to bear.
Accept these gifts to deck her body, bury them

with her. Oh yes, she well deserves honor in death.
She died to save your life, my son. She would not let   620
me be a childless old man, would not let me waste
away in sorrowful age deprived of you. Thereby,
daring this generous action, she has made the life
of all women become a thing of better repute
than it was.

              O you who saved him, you who raised us up   625
when we were fallen, farewell, even in Hades' house
may good befall you.

              I say people ought to marry women
like this. Otherwise, better not to marry at all.

ADMETUS

I never invited you to come and see her buried,
nor do I count your company as that of a friend.   630
She shall not wear anything that you bring her.
She needs nothing from you to be buried in. Your time
to share my sorrow was when I was about to die.
But you stood out of the way and let youth take my place
in death, though you were old. Will you cry for her now?   635
It cannot be that my body ever came from you,
nor did the woman who claims she bore me and is called
my mother give me birth. I was got from some slave
and surreptitiously put to your wife to nurse.
You show it. Your nature in the crisis has come out.   640
I do not count myself as any child of yours.
Oh, you outpass the cowardice of all the world,
you at your age, come to the very last step of life
and would not, dared not, die for your own child. Oh no,
you let this woman, married into our family,   645
do it instead, and therefore it is right for me
to call her all the father and mother that I have.
And yet you two should honorably have striven for
the right of dying for your child. The time of life
you had left for your living was short, in any case,   650

and she and I would still be living out our time°
and I should not be hurt and grieving over her.
And yet, all that a man could have to bless his life
you have had. You had your youth in kingship. There was I
your son, ready to take it over, keep your house   655
in order, so you had no childless death to fear,
with the house left to be torn apart by other claims.
You cannot justify your leaving me to death
on grounds that I disrespected your old age. Always I
showed all consideration. See what thanks I get   660
from you and from the woman who gave me birth. Go on,
get you other children—you cannot do it too soon—
who will look after your old age, and lay you out
when you are dead, and see you buried properly.
I will not do it. This hand will never bury you.   665
I am dead as far as you are concerned, and if, because
I found another savior, I still look on the sun,
I count myself that person's child and fond support.
It is meaningless, the way the old men pray for death
and complain of age and the long time they have to live.   670
Let death only come close, not one of them still wants
to die. Their age is not a burden any more.

CHORUS LEADER

Stop, stop. We have trouble enough already, child.
You will exasperate your father with this talk.

PHERES

Big words, son. Who do you think you are cursing out   675
like this? Some Lydian slave, some Phrygian that you bought?
I am a free Thessalian noble, nobly born
from a Thessalian. Are you forgetting that? You go
too far with your high-handedness. You volley brash
words at me, and fail to hit me, and then run away.   680
I gave you life, and made you master of my house,
and raised you. I am not obliged to die for you.
I do not acknowledge any tradition among us

that fathers should die for their sons. That is not Greek either.
Your natural right is to find your own happiness   685
or unhappiness. All you deserve from me, you have.
You are lord of many. I have wide estates of land
to leave you, just as my father left them to me.
What harm have I done you then? What am I taking away
from you? Do not die for me, I will not die for you.   690
You like the sunlight. Don't you think your father does?
I count the time I have to spend down there as long,
and the time to live is little, but that little is sweet.
You fought shamelessly for a way to escape death,
and passed your proper moment, and are still alive   695
because you killed her. Then, you wretch, you dare to call
me coward, when you let your woman outdare you,
and die for her magnificent young man? I see.
You have found a clever scheme by which you *never* will die.
You will always persuade the wife you have at the time   700
to die for you instead. And you, so low, then dare
blame your own people for not wanting to do this.
Silence. I tell you, as you cherish your own life,
all other people cherish theirs. And if you call
us names, you will be called names, and the names are true.   705

CHORUS LEADER
Too much evil has been said in this speech and in
that spoken before. Old sir, stop cursing your own son.

ADMETUS
No, speak, as I have spoken.° If it hurts to hear
the truth, you should not have made a mistake with me.

PHERES
I should have made a mistake if I had died for you.   710

ADMETUS
Is it the same thing to die old and to die young?

PHERES

Yes. We have only one life and not two to live.

ADMETUS

I think you would like to live a longer time than Zeus.

PHERES

Cursing your parents, when they have done you no wrong?

ADMETUS

Yes, for I found you much in love with a long life.   715

PHERES

Who is it you are burying? Did not someone die?

ADMETUS

And that she died, you foul wretch, proves your cowardice.

PHERES

You cannot say that we were involved in her death.

ADMETUS

Ah.
I hope that some day you will stand in need of me.   720

PHERES

Go on, and court more women, so they all can die.

ADMETUS

Your fault. You were not willing to die.

PHERES

                                        No, I was not.
It is a sweet thing, this god's sunshine, sweet to see.

ADMETUS

That is an abject spirit, not a man's.

PHERES

                                        You shall
not mock an old man while you carry out your dead.

ADMETUS

You will die in evil memory, when you do die.   725

PHERES

I do not care what they say of me when I am dead.

ADMETUS

How old age loses all the sense of shame.

PHERES

                                        She was
not shameless, the woman you found; she was only stupid.

ADMETUS

Get out of here now and let me bury my dead.

PHERES

I'll go. You murdered her, and you can bury her.   730
But you will have her brothers still to face. You'll pay,
for Acastus is no longer counted as a man
unless he sees you punished for his sister's blood.

ADMETUS

Go and be damned, you and that woman who lives with you.
Grow old as you deserve, childless, although your son   735
still lives. You shall not come again under the same roof
with me. And if I had to proclaim by heralds that I
disown my father's house, I should have so proclaimed.

                                    (*Exit Pheres to the side.*)

Now we, for we must bear the sorrow that is ours,
shall go, and lay her body on the burning place.   740

CHORUS [*chanting*]

Ah, cruel the price of your daring,
O generous one, O noble and brave,
farewell. May Hermes of the world below
and Hades welcome you. And if, even there,
the good fare best, may you have high honor   745
and sit by the bride of Hades.

(Exit all to the side. The stage is empty. Enter a Servant from the house.)

SERVANT

I have known all sorts of foreigners who have come in
from all over the world here to Admetus' house,
and I have served them dinner, but I never yet
have had a guest as bad as this to entertain.   750
In the first place, he could see the master was in mourning,
but inconsiderately came in anyway.
Then, he refused to understand the situation
and be content with anything we could provide,
but when we failed to bring him something, demanded it,   755
and took a cup with ivy on it in both hands
and drank the wine of our dark mother, straight, until
the flame of the wine went all through him, and heated him,
and then he wreathed branches of myrtle on his head
and howled, off-key. There were two kinds of music now   760
to hear, for while he sang and never gave a thought
to the sorrows of Admetus' house, we servants were
    mourning
our mistress; but we could not show before our guest
with our eyes wet. Admetus had forbidden that.
So now I have to entertain this guest inside,   765
this ruffian thief, this highwayman, whoever he is,
while she is gone away from the house, and I could not
say good-bye, stretch my hand out to her in my grief
for a mistress who was like a mother to all the house
and me. She gentled her husband's rages, saved us all   770
from trouble after trouble. Am I not then right
to hate this guest who has come here in our miseries?

(Enter Heracles from the house, drunk.)

HERACLES

You there, with the sad and melancholy face, what is
the matter with you? The servant who looks after guests
should be polite and cheerful and not scowl at them.   775

But look at you. Here comes your master's dearest friend
to visit you, and you receive him with black looks
and frowns, all because of trouble in someone else's family.
Come here, I'll tell you something that will make you wiser.
Do you really know what life is like, the way it is?   780
I don't think so. How could you? Well then, listen to me.
Death is an obligation that we all must pay.
There is not one man living who can truly say
if he will be alive or dead on the next day.
Fortune is dark; she moves, but we cannot see the way   785
nor can we pin her down by expertise and study her.
There, I have told you. Now you can understand. Go on,
enjoy yourself, drink, call the life you live today
your own, but only that; the rest belongs to chance.
Then, beyond all gods, pay your best attentions to   790
Cypris, man's sweetest. There's a god who's kind.
Let everything else go and do as I prescribe
for you, that is, if I seem to talk sense. Do I?
I think so. Well, then, get rid of this too-much grief,
put flowers on your head and drink with us, fight down   795
these present troubles;° later, I know very well
that the wine splashing in the bowl will shake you loose
from these scowl-faced looks and the tension in your mind.
We are only human. Our thoughts should be human too,
since, for these solemn people and these people who scowl,   800
the whole parcel of them, if I am any judge,
life is not really life but a catastrophe.

SERVANT

I know all that. But we have troubles on our hands
now that make revelry and laughter out of place.

HERACLES

The dead woman is out of the family. Do not mourn   805
too hard. Your master and mistress are alive.

SERVANT

What do you mean, alive? Don't you know what happened
   to us?

HERACLES

Certainly, unless your master has lied to me.

SERVANT

He is too hospitable, too much.

HERACLES

                                   Should I not then
have enjoyed myself, because some outside woman was dead?   810

SERVANT

She was an outsider indeed. That is too true.

HERACLES

Has something happened that he did not tell me about?

SERVANT

Never mind. Go. Our masters' sorrows are our own.

HERACLES

These can be no outsiders' troubles.

SERVANT

                                   If they were,
I should not have minded seeing you enjoy yourself.   815

HERACLES

Have I been scandalously misled by my own friends?

SERVANT

You came here when we were not prepared to take in guests.
You see, we are in mourning. You can see our robes°
of black, and how our hair is cut short.

HERACLES

                                   Who is dead?
The aged father? Or is one of the children gone?   820

SERVANT

My lord, Admetus' wife is dead.

HERACLES

What are you saying?
And all this time you were making me comfortable?

SERVANT

He was embarrassed to turn you from this house of his.

HERACLES

My poor Admetus, what a helpmeet you have lost!

SERVANT

We are all dead and done for now, not only she.   825

HERACLES

I really knew it when I saw the tears in his eyes,
his shorn hair and his face; but he persuaded me
with talk of burying someone who was not by blood
related. So, unwillingly, I came inside
and drank here in the house of this hospitable man   830
when he was in this trouble! Worse, I wreathed my head
with garlands, and drank freely. But you might have said
something about this great disaster in the house.
Now, where shall I find her? Where is the funeral being held?

SERVANT

Go straight along the Larisa road, and when you clear   835
the city you will see the monument and the mound.

(Exit the Servant into the house.)

HERACLES

O heart of mine and hand of mine, who have endured
so much already, prove what kind of son it was
Alcmene, daughter of Electryon, bore to Zeus
in Tiryns. I must save this woman who has died   840
so lately, bring Alcestis back to live in this house,
and pay Admetus all the kindness that I owe.

I must go there and watch for Death of the black robes,
master of dead men, and I think I shall find him
drinking the blood of slaughtered beasts beside the grave.   845
Then, if I can break suddenly from my hiding place,
catch him, and hold him in the circle of these arms,
there is no one who will be able to break my hold
on his bruised ribs, until he gives the woman up
to me. But if I miss my quarry, if he does not come   850
to the bloody offering, I will go down, I will ask
the Maiden and the Master in the sunless homes
of those below; and I have confidence I shall bring
Alcestis back up, and give her to the arms of my friend
who did not drive me off but took me into his house   855
and, though he staggered under the stroke of circumstance,
hid it, for he was noble and respected me.
Who in all Thessaly is a truer friend than this?
Who in all Greece? Therefore, he must not ever say
that, being noble, he befriended a worthless man.   860

(Exit Heracles to the side. Then enter Admetus from
the side, accompanied by the Chorus.)

ADMETUS [*chanting*]
Hateful is this
return, hateful the sight of this house
widowed, empty. Where shall I go?
Where shall I stay? What shall I say?
How can I die?
My mother bore me to a heavy fate.   865
I envy the dead. I long for those
who are gone, to live in their houses, with them.
There is no pleasure in the sunshine
nor the feel of the hard earth under my feet.
Such was the hostage Death has taken   870
from me, and given to Hades.

(While the Chorus sings, Admetus moans inarticulately.)

CHORUS

Go on, go on. Plunge in the deep of the house.
What you have suffered is enough for tears.
You have gone through pain, I know,
but you do no good to the woman who lies   875
below. Never again to look on the face
of the wife you loved hurts you.

ADMETUS [now chanting]
You have opened the wound torn in my heart.
What can be worse for a man than to lose
a faithful wife. I envy those   880
without wives, without children. I wish I had not
ever married her, lived with her in this house.
We have each one life. To grieve for this
is burden enough.
When we could live single all our days   885
without children, it is not to be endured
to see children sicken or married love
despoiled by death.

        (As before: while the Chorus sings, Admetus moans inarticulately.)

CHORUS

ANTISTROPHE A
Chance comes. It is hard to wrestle against it.
There is no limit to set on your pain.   890
The weight is heavy. Yet still
bear up. You are not the first man to lose
his wife. Disaster appears, to crush
one man now, but afterward another.

ADMETUS [chanting]
How long my sorrows, the pain for my loves   895
down under the earth.
Why did you stop me from throwing myself

in the hollow cut of the grave, there to lie
dead beside her, who was best on earth?
Then Hades would have held fast two lives,   900
not one, and the truest of all, who crossed
the lake of the dead together.

CHORUS [*singing*]

STROPHE B

There was a man
of my people, who lost a boy
in his house anyone would mourn for,   905
the only child. But still
he bore the evil well enough, though childless,
and he stricken with age
and the hair gray on him,
well on in his lifetime.   910

ADMETUS [*chanting*]

O builded house, how shall I enter you?
How dwell in you, with this new turn
of my fortune? How different now and then.
Then it was with Pelian pine torches,   915
with marriage songs, that I entered my house,
with the hand of a sweet bride on my arm,
with loud rout of revelers following
to bless her who now is dead, and me,
for our high birth, for nobilities   920
from either side which were joined in us.
Now the bridal chorus has changed for a dirge,
and for white robes the costumed black
goes with me inside
to where our room stands deserted.   925

CHORUS [*singing*]

ANTISTROPHE B

Your luck had been
good, so you were inexperienced when

this grief came. Still you saved
your own life and being.
Your wife is dead, your love forsaken.   930
What is new in this? Before
now death has parted
many from their wives.

ADMETUS [*now speaking*]
Friends, I believe my wife is happier than I   935
although I know she does not seem to be. For her,
there will be no more pain to touch her ever again.
She has her glory and is free from much distress.
But I, who should not be alive, who have passed by
my moment, shall lead a sorry life. I see it now.   940
How can I bear to go inside this house again?
Whom shall I speak to? Who will speak to me, to give
me any pleasure in coming home? Where shall I turn?
The desolation in my house will drive me out
when I see my wife's bed empty, when I see the chairs   945
she used to sit in, and all about the house the floor
unwashed and dirty, while the children at my knees
huddle and cry for their mother and the servants mourn
their mistress and remember what the house has lost.
So it will be at home, but if I go outside   950
meeting my married friends in Thessaly, the sight
of their wives will drive me back, for I cannot endure
to look at my wife's age-mates and the friends of her youth.
And anyone who hates me will say this of me:
"Look at the man, disgracefully alive, who dared   955
not die, but like a coward gave his wife instead
and so escaped death. Do you call him a man at all?
He turns on his own parents, but he would not die
himself." Besides my other troubles, they will speak
about me thus. What have I gained by living, friends,   960
when reputation, life, and action all are bad?

CHORUS [*singing*]

I myself, in the transports
of mystic verses, as in study
of history and science, have found
nothing so strong as Compulsion,   965
nor any means to combat her,
not in the Thracian books set down
in verse by the voice of Orpheus,
not in all the remedies Phoebus has given the heirs   970
of Asclepius to fight the many afflictions of man.

ANTISTROPHE A

She alone is a goddess
without altar or statue to pray
before. She heeds no sacrifice.   975
Majesty, bear no harder
on me than you have in my life before!
All Zeus himself ordains
only with you is accomplished.
By strength you fold and crumple the steel of the Chalybes.   980
There is no pity in the sheer barrier of your will.

STROPHE B

Now the goddess has caught you in the breakless grip of her hands.
Bear up. You will never bring back up, by crying,   985
the dead into the light again.
Even the sons of the gods fade
and go in death's shadow.   990
She was loved when she was with us.
She shall be loved still, now she is dead.
It was the best of all women to whom you were joined in marriage.

ANTISTROPHE B

The monument of your wife must not be counted among the graves 995
of the dead, but it must be given honors

like the gods' worship of wayfarers.
And as they turn the bend of the road   1000
and see it, men shall say:
"She died for the sake of her husband.
Now she is a blessed spirit.
Hail, majesty, be gracious to us." Thus will men speak in her
   presence.   1005

CHORUS LEADER
But here is someone who looks like Alcmene's son,
Admetus. He seems on his way to visit you.

(Enter Heracles from the side, leading a veiled woman.)

HERACLES
A man, Admetus, should be allowed to speak freely
to a friend, instead of keeping his complaints suppressed
inside him. Now, I thought I had the right to stand   1010
beside you and endure what you endured, so prove
my friendship. But you never told me that she, who lay
dead, was your wife, but entertained me in your house
as if your mourning were for some outsider's death.
And so I wreathed my head and poured libations out   1015
to the gods, in your house, though your house had
   suffered so.
This was wrong, wrong I tell you, to have treated me
thus, though I have no wish to hurt you in your grief.
Now, as for the matter of why I have come back again,
I will tell you. Take this woman, keep her safe for me,   1020
until I have killed the master of the Bistones
and come back, bringing with me the horses of Thrace.
If I have bad luck—I hope not, I hope to come
back home—I give her to the service of your house.
It cost a struggle for her to come into my hands.   1025
You see, I came on people who were holding games
for all comers, with prizes which an athlete might
well spend an effort winning.

(Points to the woman.)

                                    Here is the prize I won
and bring you. For the winners in the minor events
were given horses to take away, while those who won   1030
the heavier stuff, boxing and wrestling, got oxen,
and a woman was thrown in with them. Since I happened
to be there, it seemed wrong to let this splendid prize
go by. As I said, the woman is for you to keep.
She is not stolen. It cost me hard work to bring   1035
her here. Some day, perhaps, you will say I have done well.

ADMETUS

I did not mean to dishonor nor belittle you
when I concealed the fate of my unhappy wife,
but it would have added pain to pain already there
if you had been driven to shelter with some other host.   1040
This sorrow is mine. It is enough for me to weep.
As for the woman, if it can be done, my lord,
I beg you, have some other Thessalian, who has not
suffered as I have, keep her. You have many friends
in Pherae. Do not bring my sorrows back to me.   1045
I would not have strength to see her in my house and keep
my eyes dry. I suffer now. Do not inflict further
suffering on me. I have sorrow enough to weigh me down.
And where could a young woman live in this house? For
she is young, I can see it in her dress, her style.   1050
Am I to put her in the same quarters with the men?
And how, circulating among young men, shall she be kept
from harm? Not easy, Heracles, to hold in check
a young strong man. I am thinking of your interests.
Or shall I put her in my lost wife's chamber, keep   1055
her there? How can I take her to Alcestis' bed?
I fear blame from two quarters, from my countrymen
who might accuse me of betraying her who helped
me most, by running to the bed of another girl,
and from the dead herself. Her honor has its claim   1060

on me. I must be very careful. You, lady,
whoever you are, I tell you that you have the same
form as my Alcestis; all your body is like hers.
Too much. Oh, by the gods, take this woman away
out of my sight. I am beaten already, do not beat   1065
me again. For as I look on her, I think I see
my wife. It churns my heart to tumult, and the tears
break streaming from my eyes. How much must I endure
the bitter taste of sorrow which is still so fresh?

CHORUS LEADER

I cannot put a good name to your fortune; yet   1070
whoever you are, you must endure what the god gives.

HERACLES

I only wish that my strength had been great enough
for me to bring your wife back from the chambered deep
into the light. I would have done that grace for you.

ADMETUS

I know you would have wanted to. Why speak of it?   1075
There is no way for the dead to come back to the light.

HERACLES

Then do not push your sorrow. Bear it as you must.

ADMETUS

Easier to comfort than to suffer and be strong.

HERACLES

But if you wish to mourn forever, what will you gain?

ADMETUS

Nothing. I know it. But some impulse of my love   1080
makes me.

HERACLES

        Why, surely. Love for the dead is cause for tears.

ADMETUS

Her death destroyed me, even more than I can say.

HERACLES

You have lost a fine wife. Who will say you have not?

ADMETUS

So fine

that I, whom you see, never shall enjoy life again.

HERACLES

Time will soften the evil. It still is young and strong.   1085

ADMETUS

You can say time will soften it, if time means death.

HERACLES

A wife, your new marriage will put an end to this desire.

ADMETUS

Silence! I never thought you would say a thing like that.

HERACLES

What? You will not remarry but keep an empty bed?

ADMETUS

No woman ever shall sleep in my arms again.   1090

HERACLES

Do you believe you help the dead by doing this?

ADMETUS

Wherever she may be, she deserves my honors still.

HERACLES

Praiseworthy, yes, praiseworthy. And yet foolish, too.

ADMETUS

Call me so, then, but never call me a bridegroom.

HERACLES

I admire you for your faith and love you bear your wife.   1095

ADMETUS

Let me die if I betray her, though she is gone.

HERACLES

Well then,
receive this woman into your most generous house.

ADMETUS

Please, in the name of Zeus your father, no!

HERACLES

And yet
you will be making a mistake if you do not.

ADMETUS

And I'll be eaten at the heart with anguish if I do.   1100

HERACLES

Obey. The grace of this may come where you need grace.

ADMETUS

Ah.
I wish you had never won her in those games of yours.

HERACLES

Where I am winner, you are winner along with me.

ADMETUS

Honorably said. But let the woman go away.

HERACLES

She will go, if she should. First look. See if she should.   1105

ADMETUS

She should, unless it means you will be angry with me.

HERACLES

Something I know of makes me so insistent with you.

ADMETUS

So, win again. But what you do does not please me.

HERACLES

The time will come when you will thank me. Only obey.

ADMETUS   (*To attendants.*)

Escort her in, if she must be taken into this house.   1110

HERACLES

I will not hand this lady over to attendants.

ADMETUS

You yourself lead her into the house then, if you wish.

HERACLES

I will put her into your hands and into yours alone.

ADMETUS

I will not touch her. But she is free to come inside.

HERACLES

No, I have faith in your right hand, and only yours.   1115

ADMETUS

My lord, you are forcing me to act against my wish.

HERACLES

Be brave. Reach out your hand and touch the stranger.

ADMETUS

                                                        So.

Here is my hand; I feel like Perseus killing the Gorgon.

HERACLES

You have her?

ADMETUS

                Yes, I have her.

HERACLES

                                Keep her, then. Some day
you will say the son of Zeus came as your generous guest.   1120
But look at her. See if she does not seem most like
your wife. Your grief is over now. Your luck is back.

ADMETUS

Gods, what shall I think! Amazement beyond hope, as I

look on this woman, this wife. Is she really mine,
or some sweet mockery for a god to stun me with?   1125

HERACLES

Not so. This is your own wife you see. She is here.

ADMETUS

Be careful she is not some phantom from the depths.

HERACLES

The guest and friend you took was no necromancer.

ADMETUS

Do I see my wife, whom I was laying in the grave?

HERACLES

Surely. But I do not wonder at your unbelief.   1130

ADMETUS

May I touch her, and speak to her, as my living wife?

HERACLES

Speak to her. All that you desired is yours.

ADMETUS

                                        Oh, eyes
and body of my dearest wife, I have you now
beyond all hope. I never thought I'd see you again.

HERACLES

You have her. May no god begrudge you your happiness.   1135

ADMETUS

O nobly sprung child of all-highest Zeus, may good
fortune go with you. May the father who gave you birth
keep you safe. You alone raised me up when I was down.
How did you bring her back from down there to the light?

HERACLES

I fought a certain deity who had charge of her.   1140

ADMETUS

Where do you say you fought this match with Death?

HERACLES

                                         Beside

the tomb itself. I ambushed him and caught him in my
    hands.

ADMETUS

But why is my wife standing here, and does not speak?

HERACLES

You are not allowed to hear her speak to you until
her obligations to the gods who live below   1145
are washed away and the third morning comes. So now
take her and lead her inside, and for the rest of time,
Admetus, be just: treat your guests as they deserve.
And now good-bye. I have my work that I must do,
and go to face the lordly son of Sthenelus.   1150

ADMETUS

No, stay with us and be the guest of our hearth.

HERACLES

                                  There still

will be a time for that, but I must press on now.

ADMETUS

Success go with you. May you find your way back here.

(Exit Heracles to the side.)

I proclaim to all the people of my tetrarchy
that, for these blessed happenings, they shall set up
dances, and the altars smoke with sacrifice offered.   1155
For now we shall make our life again, and it will be
a better one.
            I was lucky. That I cannot deny.

(Exit with Alcestis into the house.)

CHORUS [*chanting*]
Many are the forms of what is divine.

Much that the gods achieve is surprise.　　　　　　　　　　
What we look for does not come to pass;
a god finds a way for what none foresaw.
Such was the end of this story.

(Exit all.)

MEDEA

Translated by OLIVER TAPLIN

MEDEA: INTRODUCTION

The Play: Date and Composition

Euripides' *Medea* was produced in 431 BCE as the first of his four plays entered in the annual dramatic competition. The other plays have been lost: *Philoctetes*, *Dictys*, and the satyr-play *Theristae* (*The Mowers*). Euripides took the third prize. Although *Medea* is one of his earliest securely dated plays to survive, he was probably over fifty years old when he wrote it and had already been competing in the dramatic contests for more than twenty years.

Some ancient scholars report that, according to Aristotle and his student Dicaearchus (fourth century BCE), Euripides revised a play called *Medea* by a certain Neophron (a prolific and successful rival Athenian dramatist) and passed it off as his own; a few even claimed that Euripides' *Medea* was in fact completely the work of Neophron and should be attributed to him. Various ancient commentaries cite passages from Neophron's *Medea* adding up to about twenty-four lines; these do not coincide exactly with Euripides' play, but they are very similar in content. Modern scholars are divided about what to make of all this: some think that Neophron's *Medea* did indeed precede and influence Euripides'; others have maintained instead that Neophron's play came later and that those who thought otherwise in antiquity were mistaken.

The Myth

Medea is a well-known figure from archaic Greek epic and legend. Her name is derived from words meaning "counsel, plan, cleverness." Grand-daughter of Helios (god of the sun), she possesses magic powers with which she can help or harm male heroes. In this regard she is similar to her aunt Circe. In some versions of the myth, Medea is a goddess, in others a human. She plays a crucial role in the popular ancient Greek epic stories that told how the Argonauts, led by Jason, sailed to far-off Colchis on the Black Sea and overcame various challenges and obstacles in order to bring back the Golden Fleece with them to Greece—all aided decisively by Medea, who, out of love for Jason, betrayed her own family (the rulers of Colchis and guardians of the Fleece) and chose to put her sorcery at his service. It was through her powers and advice that Jason succeeded in putting a dragon to sleep and killing it, then harnessed fierce oxen with which he plowed furrows to sow the dragon's teeth, killed the armed men who sprang up from the teeth he had sown, and then managed to escape from Colchis and avenge himself on his enemies.

After Jason and Medea escaped they took up residence in Corinth, where they had children together. But Jason subsequently decided instead to marry the daughter of the king of Corinth (Creon). It is here that the action of Euripides' *Medea* begins: we see how Medea kills this new bride and her father and the children she had had with Jason, and then escapes from Corinth to Athens. Various ancient poets and local historians, some of them writing before Euripides, mentioned the death of Jason and Medea's children at Corinth—the local cult in which they were honored there is well attested—but gave different explanations for just how the children had died: that the Corinthians murdered the boys in a temple of Hera out of hatred for Medea; or that, after Medea had killed Creon and fled to Athens, leaving her children at the temple of Hera, Creon's relatives avenged themselves by killing the children; or that Medea tried to make the children immortal but something went wrong and they died. The idea that Medea deliberately killed her own children may or may not have been a new invention by Euripides (or Neophron).

After the events in Corinth, Medea goes on to Athens, where she marries King Aegeus and (in some versions) tries to kill his son Theseus. Years later she returns to her homeland Colchis, where she becomes queen. According to some versions, she ends up marrying Achilles after their deaths and reigning with him over the souls of the dead.

Euripides seems to have been particularly interested in Medea: before he composed this play he had already dramatized two other episodes from the myths involving her, one about earlier events (*The Daughters of Pelias*) and one about later ones (*Aegeus*). But both of these plays are lost.

Transmission and Reception

Although *Medea* was not particularly successful when it was first produced, it went on to become enormously popular and influential. It belongs to the group of ten plays by Euripides that were most widely diffused during ancient and medieval times. Its popularity among ancient readers is attested by a dozen papyrus fragments dating from the third century BCE to the sixth century CE. So it is perhaps not surprising that modern scholars have detected what seem to be numerous small interpolations in the text, probably due in some cases to expansion by directors or actors—further evidence for the play's continuing vitality on ancient stages.

Euripides' *Medea* exerted considerable influence upon later Greek and Roman versions of the story. Of Roman tragedies, we possess Seneca's *Medea* and know that Ovid wrote a highly regarded *Medea*, now lost. And the influence of Euripides' play is no less evident in such Greek and Roman narrative epics as Apollonius of Rhodes' *Argonautica*, Ovid's *Metamorphoses*, and Valerius Flaccus' *Argonautica*. Most ancient versions of the Medea story emphasize her magic powers and concentrate on her more terrifying aspects. On south Italian vase paintings of the fourth and third centuries BCE, several of them clearly influenced by theatrical productions, Medea is often displayed killing her children or escaping with their bodies on her winged chariot. Pompeian frescoes show her anguished indecision about whether or not to kill the children. Later Roman sarcophagi frequently depict the terrible death of Creon's daughter and Medea's spectacular escape.

In modern times *Medea* has become one of the very best known of all ancient tragedies. The story of the woman who avenges herself upon her unfaithful husband by killing their children has become part of the popular imagination and has played an important role in such fields as politics (Medea's monologue on the troubles of women was cited regularly in meetings of the British suffragettes), psychoanalysis, and law. Besides the frequent productions of Euripides' play on stages throughout the world in all languages, including ancient Greek—probably no other ancient play has been produced anywhere near as often in the twentieth century—the story has also inspired numerous new versions, including Franz Grillparzer's dramatic trilogy *The Golden Fleece* (1819-21), Christa Wolf's novel *Medea.Voices* (1996), Luigi Cherubini's opera *Medea* (1797), Martha Graham's dance drama *Cave of the Heart* (1946, with music by Samuel Barber), and films by Pier Paolo Pasolini (1969) and Lars von Trier (1988). It has also been depicted in important paintings (Eugène Delacroix, 1862; Gustave Moreau, 1865) and sculptures (Auguste Rodin, 1865-70).

MEDEA

Scene: Corinth, in front of Medea's house.

                            (Enter Nurse from the house.)

NURSE
   If only the swift *Argo* never had swooped in between
   the cobalt Clashing Rocks to reach the Colchians' realm;
   if only pines had never been chopped down among the
     woods
   of Pelion to put oars in the hands of those heroic men,
   who ventured forth to fetch the Golden Fleece for Pelias.   5
   Medea, then, my mistress, never would have sailed
   for Iolcus' towers, her heart infatuated with desire for Jason;
   nor spurred the daughters of old Pelias to kill their father,
   never would have settled here in Corinth   10
   with her husband and her sons.
   She managed though an exile° to delight the people of the
     land

she'd joined, and gave support in every way to Jason—
life's most secure when there is no conflict
to alienate a woman from her man.   15
But now . . . now hatred rules, and loyal love is sick,
since Jason has betrayed my mistress and their sons,
by mounting the royal bridal bed
beside the daughter of Creon, the monarch of this land.
And so my poor Medea is disdained.   20
She cries, "What of his oaths?," recalls
the solemn pledge of his right hand, and prays the gods
to witness what poor recompense she has received.
Lying without food, she gives her body up to pain,
and has been wearing down the nights and days with tears,   25
since she first found she had been wrongly treated by her
    man.
Never lifting up her eyes from staring at the ground,
she listens to her friends' advice no more
than if she were a rock or sea-surf—
except for when she turns her pale white neck,   30
lamenting to herself for her lost father, country, home,
which she betrayed to join the man who now dishonors her.
She's learned from her catastrophe how much
it matters not to lose your homeland.   35
She hates the children, takes no pleasure in the sight of them.°
I fear that she may plan some new mischief;
her temperament is fierce, and she'll not tolerate
mistreatment—I know too well what she is like.
She fills me with alarm,
that she will stab their livers with a sharpened sword,°   40
entering by stealth the palace where the bed is laid,
and kill both monarch and his daughter's new bridegroom,
and so incur some even graver consequence,
for she is fearsome—
and no one who picks a fight with her
will find it easy to descant the victory chant.   45

(Enter the two boys and their Tutor from the side.)

But here the children come, fresh from their exercise,
and unaware of all their mother's sufferings—
young minds are not inclined to cares.

TUTOR

Old servant of my mistress' house,
why are you standing solitary here outside the doors,
bewailing troubles to yourself?   50
How could Medea want to be left without you near?

NURSE

Old man, you who take care of the young sons of Jason:
when affairs break badly for their masters,
this can affect good slaves as well.   55
And my distress reached such a pitch I felt compelled
to come out here and tell the problems that beset
my mistress to the earth and sky.

TUTOR

You mean she's still not stopped her grieving cries?

NURSE

You've no idea! Her pain's not even halfway through.   60

TUTOR

Poor fool—if I may say that of my betters—
how little she knows yet about the latest downward turn.

NURSE

What's that, old man? Don't hold it back from me.

TUTOR

Nothing—I wish I had not said a thing.

NURSE

Do not, I beg you, hide this from your fellow slave.   65
I shall keep quiet about these matters, if I should.

TUTOR

    I overheard a person say—pretending not to hear
    as I drew near to where the old men sit
    and play their checkers, by the sacred spring of Peirene—
    I heard him say that Creon, lord of this land, intends   70
    to drive these children out from Corinth, with their mother.
    I do not know whether this rumor's true—I only hope it's not.

NURSE

    Will Jason tolerate such treatment of his sons
    even if he has this feud against their mother?   75

TUTOR

    Ancient ties become displaced by newer ones;
    and he's no friend to this house here.

NURSE

    Then we are ruined if we have to add
    this new disaster to the one we've not yet drained.

TUTOR

    But you at least keep quiet and spread no word of this—   80
    it's not the time to let our mistress find this out.

NURSE

    Do you hear how your father's turned against you, children?
    I won't say "curse him," since he is my master still.
    But he has been exposed as false toward his closest kin.

TUTOR

    And who has not? Have you found out so late   85
    that every person loves himself more than those close to him,
    some justly, some for profit's sake?°
    And so the father of these boys does not feel love for them,
    because of his new bride.

NURSE   *(To the children.)*
    All will be well; now, children, go inside.

                                           (To the Tutor.)

And you should keep them well secluded 90
from their mother for so long as she remains
in such an agitated state; don't let them near.
I've seen her cast a savage look at them,
as though she's contemplating doing something to them.
I know for sure she won't relent her anger
until she's struck some victim to the ground—
but when she does, may it be enemies, not friends. 95

MEDEA [singing from inside]
Oh, in pain, in pain,
I'm so unhappy, I . . .
oh for me, for me,
if only I could die.

NURSE [chanting throughout this scene while Medea continues to sing
from inside]
As I said, dear children, your mother is stirring
her passion, bestirring her fury.
Now hurry indoors; don't stray in her sight, 100
don't even go near, keep well away
from her violent mood,
the wild hate of her passionate will.
Hurry along, quickly inside. 105
It is all too clear that she's going to ignite
this cloud of complaint now billowing
from its beginning to yet hotter resentment.
What will she do, now that her heart
has been so envenomed,
proud to its core, tough to restrain? 110

(*Exit the two boys and the Tutor into the house.*)

MEDEA (*Inside.*)
The suffering I have endured, endured,
calling for bitter lament aloud!
Accursed children of a hated mother,

I wish you were done for along with your father.
To hell with the family, all of the house.

NURSE

Oh no, terrible! Why should your children   115
share in the guilt of the crimes of their father?
Why should you hate them?
I'm utterly stricken with fear for your safety,
poor children. Rulers have dangerous natures:
subjected to little, controlling much,   120
they are not inclined to relent from their passions.
Better to live in the ways of fair-sharing:
the height of ambition for me is to live out my life
without much, but entirely secure.
The word "moderation" sounds first   125
in our speaking, and is easily best in enactment.
Exaggeration can never provide
sound balance for humans.
And if ever a god gets angered against
some household, the payoff's yet greater disaster.   130

(Enter Chorus of Corinthian women.)

CHORUS [singing throughout this scene, while the Nurse continues to
chant and Medea sings from inside]
I heard her call, I heard her cry,
Medea's pain, the Colchian.
So she has still not settled calm?
Old woman, tell. I heard her voice
from deep inside her mansion gates.   135
The sufferings of this household cause
me pain—my friendship's blended close.

NURSE

No household exists any more—it's all gone.
He is possessed by his royal embraces;   140
she is eroding her life away

deep in her chamber, my lady,
her spirit encouraged not the slightest
by any suggestion from any well-wisher.

MEDEA   (Inside.)

May lightning shatter my skull;
life no longer brings gain.   145
May I find shelter in death,
freed from this hated life.

CHORUS

STROPHE

O Zeus, Earth, and shining Sky,
do you hear the wailing cry
of the inauspicious bride?   150
Why crave for that unwanted bed,
poor woman? Death comes with all speed.
Don't pray for dying, no.
If your husband worships so   155
at his newfound marriage-couch,
don't be torn by him so much.
Zeus will be your advocate;
so don't pine away so much,
wasting for your old bedmate.

MEDEA   (Inside.)

Artemis and mighty Themis,   160
see the pain that I'm enduring,
I who had my cursed husband
tied by strong bonds of his swearing.
May I see him and his consort
and their palace ripped in pieces,
payment for the ways they dared first
to mistreat me with injustice.   165
O my father, O my city,
after killing my own brother,

in disgrace I had to leave you,
lost my fatherland forever.

NURSE

You hear her calling aloud on Themis
and on Zeus, the protector of oaths   170
binding on humans? My mistress will never
relent from her anger with some petty gesture.

CHORUS

ANTISTROPHE

I wish she would meet with us,
and engage us face to face;
I wish she would heed our voice
to see if she might relent   175
from her heavy-hearted rage
and the passion of her heart.
May I never stand apart
from supporting my own friends.
But, you, please return indoors,
fetch her, bring her here outside,   180
tell her we are on her side;
quick, before she does some harm
against those inside her home—
because her intense distress
comes upon her at a pace.

NURSE

I'll do this—although I'm afraid
that I'll never prevail on my mistress—   185
I'll try as a favor.
Yet she glares like a lioness with new cubs
at anyone who comes close and offers her any suggestion.
You'd be right to conclude that the people   190
of olden times were stupid and lacking in wisdom
when they invented poems
to accompany feasts, celebrations, and dinners,

sweet ornamentations of life.
Still no one has found out the way
to abolish our harrowing griefs 195
with poetic powers
or with songs and elaborate strings—
griefs that result in the deaths and terrible mishaps
that overturn households.
Yet that would have offered us profit:
to medicine these troubles with music.
Why bother with loudly voiced singing for nothing, 200
when feasting is garnished with pleasure?
All by itself the rich banquet provides
full satisfaction for people.

CHORUS

I have heard her tearful moans 205
and the piercing words she cries
out against that guilty husband
who betrayed their marriage ties.
She has borne unjust abuse
and she calls out aloud on Themis,
guardian of the oaths of Zeus,
oaths that ferried her to Hellas 210
over ocean's inky dark,
opening a salt-sea exit
through the daunting Black Sea's lock.

(Enter Medea from the house.)

MEDEA [*speaking*]

Women of Corinth, I have come outside to show
you have no cause to tarnish me with blame. 215
Understand: I'm all too well aware
that many people are perceived as arrogant—
some privately, others in public life—and there are those
who gather a bad name for idleness by lying low.
Do not suppose there's any justice rests

in people's eyes: they hate on sight,
before they get to know a man's real inner core,   220
although he's done no wrong to them.
And therefore foreigners should take especial care
to be in tune with the society they join—
nor would I give approval even to a native man°
who foolishly offends his fellow citizens through selfishness.
But in my case, this new and unforeseeable event   225
has befallen me and crushed my spirit,
so that I've lost delight in life—I long to die, my friends.
I realize the man who was my all in all
has now turned out to be the lowest of the low—my husband.
We women are the most beset by trials   230
of any species that has breath and power of thought.
Firstly, we are obliged to buy a husband
at excessive cost, and then accept him as
the master of our body—that is even worse.
And here's the throw that carries highest stakes: 235
is he a good catch or a bad?
For changing husbands is a blot upon
a woman's good repute; and it's not possible
to say no to the things a husband wants.
A bride, when she arrives to join new ways
and customs, needs to be a prophet to predict
the ways to deal best with her new bedmate—   240
she won't have learned that back at home.
And then . . . then if, when we have spent a deal of trouble
on these things, if then our husband lives with us
bearing the yoke without its being forced,
we have an enviable life.
But if he does not: better death.
But for a man—oh no—if ever he is irked
with those he has at home, he goes elsewhere   245
to get relief and ease his state of mind.
He turns either to some close friend or to someone his age.°
Meanwhile we women are obliged

to keep our eyes on just one person.
They, men, allege that we enjoy a life
secure from danger safe at home,
while they confront the thrusting spears of war.
That's nonsense: I would rather join   250
the battle rank of shields three times
than undergo birth-labor once.
In any case, your story's not at all the same as mine:
you have your city here, your father's house,
delight in life, and company of friends,
while I am citiless, deserted,   255
subjected to humiliation by my husband.
Manhandled from a foreign land like so much pirate loot,
here I have no mother, brother, relative,
no one to offer me a port, a refuge from catastrophe.
So I would like to ask this one small thing of you:
if I can find some means or some device   260
to make my husband pay the penalty to quit me
for the wrongs he's done, stay silent, please
—also the man who's given him his daughter, and the bride
    herself.°
Although a woman is so fearful in all other ways—
no good for battle or the sight of weaponry—
when she's been wrongly treated in the field of sex,   265
there is no other cast of mind more deadly, none.

CHORUS LEADER
   I will do this: you're justified inflicting punishment,
   Medea, on your husband. I am not surprised you feel such
       pain.

                        (Creon approaches from the side.)

   I see King Creon coming to announce some new decision.   270

CREON
   Grim scowling scourge against your husband—
   yes, that's you, Medea:

I proclaim that you must leave this land in banishment,
and take your pair of sons along with you.
And no delay allowed.
I am myself the arbiter of this decree,
and I shall not go home before I have made sure   275
I've thrown you out beyond the borders of this land.

MEDEA

Aiai!
Utter, complete catastrophe for me!
My enemies are in full sail,
and I have no accessible haven
to land me from this storm of hell.
But I'll still ask, although I am so poorly treated: say,   280
what reason have you, Creon, for expelling me like this?

CREON

I am afraid of you—no point in mincing words—
I am afraid you'll work incurable mischief
upon my daughter.
And many things combine toward this fear of mine:
you are by nature clever and well versed   285
in evil practices; and you are feeling bruised
because you've been deprived of the embraces of your man.
And I have heard—so people say—you're threatening
some act against the giver in this marriage
and the taker and the given bride.
Therefore I'm going to move before that happens.
Better to be hated by you, woman, now   290
than to be soft, and later groan for it.

MEDEA

O misery . . . not for the first time reputation's
done me harm and damaged my whole life.
A man who knows what he's about should never have
his children taught to be more clever than the norm.   295

They get a name for idleness, and only earn
resentful spite from citizens.
The stupid ones, if you bring new ideas to them,
will view you as not clever but impractical.
And if you are perceived to be superior   300
to those who are supposed to be the subtle ones,
society will brand you as a troublemaker.
I myself have shared this fate:
because I'm clever, I am resented by some people,
and in some eyes I'm idle and in others opposite to that,°
and for others I'm a nuisance.   305
Yet, in any case, I'm not so very clever . . .
But still, you say you are afraid of me . . . for what?
Becoming victim of some outrage?
No, don't be scared of me, Creon.
There is no call for me to do offence against the king.
What injury have you done me?
You gave your daughter to the man your heart proposed.
It is my husband; he's the one I hate: 310
your actions were, I think, quite sensible.
So now I don't begrudge your happy state—
go on, enjoy your wedding, and good luck to you all!
And let me live on in this country here—
since, even though I have been done injustice,
I'll hold my peace, subdued by those who have more power. 315

CREON

Your words are soothing to the ear;
but I still have a horror that inside your head
you're hatching plans for something bad.
I trust you all the less than I did previously.
A woman acting in hot blood
is easier to guard against—it is the same with men—   320
than one who's clever and stays secretive.
No—on your way immediately; don't give me speeches.

It's fixed, decided, and you have no art that can contrive
to let you stay among us here as enemy to me.

MEDEA

No, no, I beg you by your knees,
and by your newly married daughter.

CREON

Why waste your breath? You'll never change my mind.   325

MEDEA

You're going to banish me,
and feel no pang of conscience for my prayers?

CREON

I am. I don't hold you closer than my own family.

MEDEA

My fatherland, how strongly I recall you now . . .

CREON

And mine, after my children, is my closest bond.

MEDEA

Ah, passion is such a deadly ill for humankind!   330

CREON

Well, that depends upon the luck of those involved.

MEDEA

O Zeus, make no mistake about
who is responsible for all these trials.

CREON

Get out, you crazy woman, and so relieve me of my pains.

MEDEA

Your pains? I have enough of those myself.
I don't need more from you.

CREON

I'm going to get my men to march you off by force.   335

MEDEA   *(Seizing his hand.)*

No, no, please don't resort to that, I beg of you, Creon.

CREON

It's clear you're set upon an ugly squabble, woman.

MEDEA

I shall submit to banishment:
that's not the thing I'm pleading for.

CREON

Then why maintain this grip? Why not release my hand?

MEDEA

Please just allow me to remain today, one day,   340
and give me time to fix arrangements for
my banishment, and make provisions for my boys,
seeing that their father does not care enough
to organize a thing for his own sons.
Pity them—you're a father after all: it's only natural
that you should feel some kindness for them.   345
I'm not concerned about myself and exile,
but them—I weep that they're subjected to distress.

CREON

My character is not at all tyrannical;
and often I have suffered harm through my softheartedness.
So now—I'm well aware of my mistake—   350
you shall obtain this none the less.
I tell you clear, however: if the sun god's coming light
still looks upon you and your boys
within the borders of this land, it means your death.
This word of mine is irreversible.
For now, if you must stay, then stay for one day more.°   355
You can't do anything I fear.

                (Exit Creon to the side, leaving Medea with the Chorus.)

CHORUS [*chanting*]
> *Unfortunate woman!°*
> *Oh, oh, sunk in your misery,*
> *where, where on earth can you turn?*
> *to what protector, to what home, to what land*   360
> *to save you from your troubles?*
> *Some god has cast you adrift, Medea, amidst*
> *an unchartable tempest of troubles.*

MEDEA
> Everything has turned out badly—no one could deny.
> But don't suppose this is the way the course will run.   365
> There are still struggles waiting for the newlyweds,
> and for the man who made this match, big troubles still.
> Do you suppose I ever would have groveled to him now
> except to gain advantage and resource?
> I would not have spent words on him, not taken hold of him.   370
> But he has plumbed such depths of foolishness
> that, when he could have foiled my plans
> by driving me away, he's let me stay for this one day—
> the day on which I shall make dead meat of my enemies—
> all three: the father and his daughter and my husband.   375
> I have a wealth of ways to post them to their deaths,
> and I'm not sure which one to make the first, good friends.
> Should I engulf the bridal home in flames,
> or stab their livers through with whetted blade,
> employing stealth to infiltrate   380
> the chambers where their bed is laid?
> But there's this one obstruction: if I get caught
> while entering to work my plot, then I'll be put to death,
> and hand my enemies the final laugh.
> So best to take the straightest route—
> my special inborn skill in drugs—   385
> and so by potions send them off.
> So be it!
> But then what next? Suppose they're dead:

what city then will take me in?
What friend will grant asylum and a home that is secure,
providing safety for my person? There is nobody.
And so I'll bide my time a little while,
and if some stronghold that can keep me safe appears,   390
deceit and secrecy will be my means to make this kill.
If that turns out to be impossible, and I'm exposed,
then I shall take a sword, although it means my death,
and slaughter them myself.
I'll push my daring to its violent end.
For, by the mistress I revere above all, fellow worker,   395
Hecate, who has her place in the recesses of my hearth,
not one of them shall rack my heart with pain
and get away with it.
I shall make sure this match of theirs is turned
to bitter anguish; bitter also that man's
marriage arrangements and attempt to exile me.   400
So down to work, Medea,
don't relax one jot of all your expertise
in schemes and in contrivances.
On to the dreadful test; now's the time to try your mettle.
You see what your position is: you must not become
a laughingstock because of Jason's union with this Sisyphean
      dynasty.   405
You're from a noble father and descended from the Sun.
You have the expertise. What's more, we are born women.
It may be we're unqualified for deeds of virtue:
yet as the architects of every kind of mischief,
we are supremely skilled.

(Medea stays on stage.)

CHORUS [*singing*]

STROPHE A

Pure rivers are running their currents upstream,   410
order and everything's turned upside down,
the dogmas of men are exposed as mere sham,

oaths by the gods prove no longer firm ground.
The stories of women shall be about-turned,   415
so that my life shall achieve proper glory,
new value is coming for our female kind,
no longer shall slanders pollute our story.   420

ANTISTROPHE A

The poems of long-ago bards shall no more
portray us as fickle, untrustworthy friends—
bias because lord Apollo forbore
to implant his lyrics in feminine minds.   425
Otherwise we could have answered with songs,
back to the masculine sex, that long years
can easily open up tales of men's wrongs,
no less than their narratives all about ours.   430

STROPHE B

You, Medea, sailed off from
your father's house,
with your heart on fire with love;
and cut your course
in between the matching rocks
of Bosphorus' straits;   435
and you've had to treat as home
an alien place,
where you've lost your marriage bed—
no husband there.
Last, you're driven, stripped of rights,
far from this shore.

ANTISTROPHE B

Dead and gone the bonding charm
of oaths men swear;
Shame's deserted Greece and flown   440
into the air.
You, poor woman, cannot claim
a father's roof,

place to move your anchorage,
sheltered from grief.
And another woman rules
over your bed,
a royal princess, who controls
your house instead.   445

(Enter Jason from the side.)

JASON

This is far from the first time that I have observed   ~~Ode to women~~
a fiery temper is an uncontrollable disaster.
You could have held on to this place,   *first feminist*
even this house, by patiently complying with   *statement*
the plans of your superiors;
instead, all thanks to your demented rant,   450
you're getting thrown out from this land.   *Euripides places*
Not that I care about myself: you can go on abusing Jason, *it right*
calling him the worst of men indefinitely.   *before*
But after all the things you've said against the ruling family, *Jason*
count it as profit that your punishment is only exile.   *enters*
I've constantly been trying to calm down   455
the enraged ruler; and I wanted you to stay.
But you refuse to curb your stupid tongue,
forever slandering the king.
And so—exile for you.
Yet even after this I've not deserted my own kin:
I've come because I'm looking out for you,   460
woman, to make quite sure that you do not depart in poverty,
together with our boys, nor under any need.
Exile brings many disadvantages along with it—
and even if you feel the deepest hate for me,
I never could reciprocate ill will for you.

MEDEA *evil/bad*   *superlatively*
You cheating rat! That's my response to you,   *completely*   465
the lowest phrase that I can find to fit your cowardice. *bad*
You come to us, you come to us,

when you have proved yourself our most detested enemy.
to gods, to me, and all the human race.°
This is not merely daring or self-confidence,
to treat your kin despicably,   470
and then to look them in the eye.
It is the worst of all the ills that plague mankind:
sheer deadness to human decency.
Yet you did well to come—since I can speak,
and ease my spirit, by condemning you;
and you will suffer pain through hearing it.
I shall begin our story from the start.   *Greek lawcourt cases*   475
I saved your life—and all the Greeks who went aboard
the *Argo* with you are aware of that—
when you were sent to set the yoke
upon the bulls with breath of fire,
and plant the ploughland with a crop of death.   480
Meanwhile the serpent which kept sleepless watch
over the Golden Fleece, with implicating coils,
I killed—and raised for you the torchlight of survival.
By my own choice I was a traitor to my home and father,
and accompanied you to Iolcus under Pelion—
from impulse rather than from careful thought.   485
I killed off Pelias, so that he died most horribly,
at his own daughters' hands—and thus extinguished his
    whole line.
And after all these favors you have had from me,
you stinking rat, you have betrayed me,
and found a new wife for your bed—
this even though we have begotten sons.
If you had been still childless, then it might have been   490
forgivable for you to hanker for this coupling.
The trust that underlies your oaths is lost:
so I'm not sure if you believe the gods of old
no longer wield their power, or else that novel rules
are now established for mankind—

Medea structure / her prosecution / all out attack / as though / she were arguing / in a law court

since you must know full well that you 495
have not made good your oaths to me.
Ah, my right hand, the hand that you so often took,
clasping my knees, how foully you have been
exploited by a cheating coward—
and how mistakenly I aimed my hopes!
Now look, I shall consult you as a friend—
though how can I expect to gain some benefit from you?— 500
yet all the same, by being asked, you'll be exposed
as even worse. Where shall I turn now?
Maybe my father's house?—the very house and fatherland
that I betrayed for you, to travel here.
Or to the wretched daughters of King Pelias?
yes, they would give me a warm welcome back, 505
when it was I who killed their father.
For that is how I stand: object of hatred for my kin at home,
I've made the people whom I should have treated well
my enemies—all for your sake.
And as reward you made me, to be sure,
the happy woman in the eyes of many girls in Greece. 510
O yes, in you I have a husband marvelous and true—
since that is why I am to be expelled from here
to wander as a refugee, devoid of friends,
alone with my poor children, all alone.
That is a fine reproach to grace the new-made groom:
his children beggars wandering 515
along with her who saved your life.
O Zeus, you've given us the clear criteria to test
if gold is counterfeit: so why is there no stamp of guarantee
marked on the human body to discriminate which ones
among our men are fakes?

CHORUS LEADER

When those who have been close collide in conflict, 520
their anger is incurable and terrible.

JASON

It seems I'm going to have to prove myself as orator,
and, like a skillful captain, reef my sails
in to the very edge, if I'm to navigate
before your windy and unbridled talk, woman.   525
For my part, since you emphasize so much my debt to you,
it's my belief that it was Cypris
alone of gods and humans steered my voyage clear of harm.
You may well have a subtle mind,
but modesty forbids me to relate just how Desire   530
compelled you with unerring shafts to keep my body safe . . .
but I'll not go into too fine detail there.
The benefits you really did for me were well and good.
Yet in return for my survival you've received
far greater profits than you have contributed—   535
as I'll explain. First you inhabit Greece
instead of some barbarian land;
you've gotten to experience the rule of justice and the law,
without consideration for the threat of force.
The Greeks have all found out about your cleverness;
you're famous for your gifts.   540
If you inhabited the furthest fringes of the world,
then no one would have heard of you.
I would not ask for vaults of gold, or for the gift to sing
yet more melodiously than Orpheus,
unless my fortune brought me also great celebrity.
So much then for my efforts made on your behalf—   545
it was you after all embarked on this debate.
I turn now to your condemnations
of the royal match that I have made.
Concerning this I'll demonstrate that I was clever first,
second restrained, and third I've been
a constant friend to you and to my sons.   550
No, please keep quiet.
When I moved here from Iolcus land, I brought with me

a number of intractable misfortunes.
So what prescription could I have discovered
more fortunate than to win the hand, although an exile,
of the king's daughter, and to marry her?
Not, as gnaws away at you, because I came to hate   555
sleeping with you, besotted by desire for my new bride.
Nor am I set on rivalry to father many children,
since I've no complaint with those I have—they are enough.
My motive is the highest of priorities:
that is for us to live a prosperous life,
and not go short—remembering that every friend   560
will run a mile from those who are impoverished.
I wish to raise my children as befits my noble house,
and father brothers for these sons I've had by you;
to put them on a par, to unify the line,
and so achieve a happy life.
For you . . . what need of children do you have?   565
Whereas for me it cashes in a gain to benefit
my living sons through those as yet unborn.
Not bad, my long-term planning?
You would agree, if you were not so stung by thoughts of sex.
You women go so far as to believe,
as long as your sex life goes well, then everything is fine;   570
but then if some misfortune strikes the realm of bed,
you count what's best and finest as your deepest hate.
I say it should have been a possibility
for mankind to engender children from some other source,
and for the female sex not to exist.
That way there'd be no troubles spoiling human life.   575

super misogynistic

CHORUS LEADER
Jason, you've laid out a speech all sparkling
with fine embellishments, and yet in my opinion,
although I may be speaking contrary to yours,
you're doing wrong with this betrayal of your wife.

MEDEA

    I'm very different from most of humankind,
    since, in my book, the clever yet unjust speech maker   580
    should be punished with the heaviest fine.
    For, confident that he can dress injustice in fine words,
    he is emboldened to stop short of nothing.
    Yet he is not so clever as all that—
    which goes for you as well.
    So don't come all respectable and eloquent with me.
    I have one argument to knock you flat: 585
    if you were not a filthy coward, you should
    have first persuaded me to give approval
    for your knotting these new marriage ties—
    not tried to keep it secret from your kin.

JASON

    Oh yes, I think it very likely you
    would have endorsed my case quite happily,
    if I'd but mentioned this new match to you—
    considering that even now you cannot bear
    to drain away the seething rage that fills your heart.   590

MEDEA

    It was not that that led you to hold back;
    it was because a non-Greek wife would not, you thought,
    enhance your status in your later years.

JASON

    Let me make clear: my motive for espousing the royal bed
    I now possess was not the woman in it—
    but, as I've said before, the wish to keep you safe,   595
    and to beget royal siblings for my sons, a safeguard for my
        line.

MEDEA

    I would not wish to live a prosperous life
    that brings me misery;
    nor do I want prosperity that eats away my soul.

JASON

I'll tell you how to change your mind, and to be seen   600
as far more sensible: don't ever take good things
to be objectionable; and don't regard yourself
as miserable when in fact you are most fortunate.

MEDEA

Humiliate me, go ahead!
You can, since you have somewhere you can turn,
while I'm deserted and must leave this land.

JASON

That's what you chose.
Don't try to pin the blame on anyone except yourself.   605

MEDEA

What did I do? Did I betray you, then,
by getting into bed with a new wife?

JASON

No, but by calling down unholy curses on the royal house.

MEDEA

I did. I am a curse upon your house as well.

JASON

Well, I'll participate no more in these adjudications.
But if you'd like to draw upon assistance from my means   610
to help the children and yourself in exile, then say the word.
I am prepared to hand out generously,
and to send tokens to my friends elsewhere
to have them treat you well.
If you refuse this, woman, you're a fool.
Give up your angry fit, and you will be far better off.   615

MEDEA

I have no wish to beg for favors from your friends,
and I will not accept a penny, so do not offer anything to us.
Donations from a low-life cheat confer no benefit.

JASON

    Well, all the same, I call upon the gods
    to witness that I am prepared to furnish all I can   620
    to make provision for the boys and you.
    Yet in return you spurn these goods,
    and willfully you push away your friends.
    As a result your hardships will be all the worse.

MEDEA

    Just go. So long away from your bedroom,
    you must be overcome with yearning
    for your freshly bridled bride.
    Go on, perform the newlywed. Perhaps—   625
    pray god fulfill this word—perhaps this wedding
    will turn out to be a bedding that you mourn.°

                           (Exit Jason to the side. Medea stays on stage.)

CHORUS [*singing*]

                    STROPHE A

Desire that overwhelms us
with infatuation
does not encourage virtue   630
and good reputation.
If her approach is gentle,
Cypris makes life blissful,
sweetest of gods; but never
target me, great mistress;
don't draw your golden bowstring
in my direction, winging
me an unerring arrow,
tip besmeared with longing.   635

                  ANTISTROPHE A

May moderation please me—
that's the gods' best favor;
and may dread Cypris never
shake my heart with fervor;

nor bring on angry quarrels
and unending clashes,
by making me inflamed for   640
other men's embraces.
May she employ her judgment
wisely to encourage
concord, by fairly settling
women's beds in marriage.

My fatherland, my home place,   645
may I be never homeless,
have never the relentless
life story of the helpless,
most pitiable of all pains.
Before that may my death-day
dark overcome this life-day.   650
There can be no disaster
that is more destructive
than to be deprived of
your fatherland, your home place.

I see from my own witness,
not secondhand from others: 655
for you there is no city,
no friend who will feel pity,
not now that you have suffered
the worst that can be suffered.
The man who is ungracious,
may death end his disgraces;
who disrespects his dearest,   660
refusing to unfasten
the latch of honest thinking.
I never shall befriend him.

                              (Enter Aegeus from the side.)

AEGEUS

Medea, happiness to you:
there is no finer prologue known with which to greet a
    friend.

MEDEA

May you be happy also, Aegeus, offspring
of wise Pandion. Where have you come from,   665
to be passing through this country here?

AEGEUS

I've journeyed from Apollo's venerable oracle.

MEDEA

And why did you consult the prophet at earth's navel-stone?

AEGEUS

To find out how I might get children as my heirs.

MEDEA

Good heavens, have you reached your age   670
still childless?

AEGEUS

Some dispensation of the gods has left me childless, yes.

MEDEA

And do you have a wife,
or have you never known the bond of wedlock?

AEGEUS

I have a wife who shares my marriage bed.

MEDEA

And what did Phoebus say to you about begetting children?

AEGEUS

Words far too subtle for a man to fathom.   675

MEDEA

Is it permissible for me to hear the oracle?

AEGEUS

It is—it does, indeed, call for a clever mind.

MEDEA

What did it say? Enlighten me if I'm allowed to hear.

AEGEUS

It told me not to tap the wineskin's jutting spout . . .

MEDEA

Before what action, or before you reach what land?   680

AEGEUS

Before I reach my native hearth.

MEDEA

What motive then has made you sail to this land here?

AEGEUS

There is a man called Pittheus—ruler of Troezen.

MEDEA

The son of Pelops; and most reverend, they say.

AEGEUS

I wish to talk with him about the prophecy.   685

MEDEA

That's good: the man is wise,
and has experience of matters such as this.

AEGEUS

Of all my allies he's the one I hold most dear.

MEDEA

Then fare you well.
And may you get all that your heart desires.

AEGEUS

But what is this? Why are your cheeks all streaked with tears?

MEDEA

Aegeus, my husband has turned out the lowest of the low.   690

AEGEUS

What? Tell me clearly all your discontent.

MEDEA

Jason has done me wrong, although I've given him no cause.

AEGEUS

What is it that he's done? Inform me more precisely.

MEDEA

He's made another woman
mistress of his bed instead of me.

AEGEUS

I can't believe he's acted so despicably as that. 695

MEDEA

It's true. I was his dear, but now I'm disregarded.

AEGEUS

So is he seized by new desire, or does he now detest your bed?

MEDEA

Desire—so great he's not stayed loyal to his family.

AEGEUS

To hell with him, then, if he is as rotten as you say.

MEDEA

This strong desire has led to his alliance with a king. 700

AEGEUS

So who has made this match with him? Come, tell me all.

MEDEA

It's Creon, ruler of this land of Corinth.

AEGEUS

I see: then, woman, I can understand just why you feel so
hurt.

MEDEA

It is disaster for me;
and, what is more, I'm being sent in exile.

AEGEUS

Who by? That's yet another blow you tell me of.   705

MEDEA

It's Creon who is driving me to banishment from Corinth.

AEGEUS

And Jason goes along with this?
I disapprove of that as well.

MEDEA

He claims he is against . . . but still he's ready to put up
    with it.
But I implore you by this beard and by your knees—   710
I am your suppliant: take pity on me
in my misfortune, take pity.
Don't watch me turned into a refugee:
grant me asylum in your land and in your house.
And then may your desire for children meet success,
thanks to the gods, and may you end your days content.   715
You may not realize what a find you've found in me:
for I shall end your barrenness,
and I shall make you potent to seed progeny.
Such are the potions that I know.

AEGEUS

There is a host of reasons, woman,
why I am inclined to grant this favor to you.   720
First, piety to the gods; and then for the fertility
that you assure me of—I'm at my wits' end over that.
This, then, is what I offer you:
if you can once arrive safe in my country,
then I'll do my best to act as your protector there,
as would be only right.

And yet I forewarn you, woman, of this much:°   725
I am not willing to convey you from this land;
but if you can all by yourself get to my home,
then you may claim asylum.
I shall not surrender you to anyone.
But you must get yourself away
out of this country by yourself;
I wish to stay above reproach with my allies as well.   730

MEDEA

Yes, I agree. All would be well for me,
if only I could have from you some surety of this.

AEGEUS

Can you distrust me? What is disconcerting you?

MEDEA

I trust you; but the house of Pelias remains my enemy,
and so is Creon. If you are tied by oath,   735
you would not let them take me from your land,
but if you were agreed with only words,
without an oath sworn by the gods,
you might become on friendly terms with them,
and then comply with their demands for extradition.
For I have no power,
while they are rich, and members of a royal house.   740

AEGEUS

The things you say show ample foresight.
So if you think it best, I'll not refuse to do this thing,
since for me it's safer if I demonstrate
to your opponents that I have good reasons,
while for you your interests gain more security.   745
Tell me the gods to be sworn by.

MEDEA

Then swear by Earth and by the Sun,
my father's father, and the whole pantheon together.

AEGEUS

What to do, what not to do? Go on.

MEDEA

That you will never cast me from your land;
and never, if one of my enemies attempts to take me,   750
never, while you live, abandon me of your free will.

AEGEUS

I swear by Earth and by the pure light of Sun
and all the gods: I shall stay true to all you say.

MEDEA

Enough. But if you fail to keep your oath,
what then should be your fate?

AEGEUS

Those things that are inflicted on the impious.   755

MEDEA

Then go, and fare you well. For everything's in place.
And as for me, I'll reach your land as quickly as I can,
once I have carried through my plans,
and gained the things I want.

CHORUS LEADER [*chanting*]
May Hermes, the patron of travelers,
usher you safely home;   760
and may you achieve those things
which you so strongly desire,
because you appear to us, Aegeus,
as a man of true nobility.

(*Exit Aegeus to the side.*)

MEDEA

O Zeus and Justice, child of Zeus, and radiance of the Sun—
now, friends, I'll win the victory against my enemies.   765
I have set out upon the road; and now I have good hope

that they shall pay the price in full.
For in the very place I was most laboring,
this man has now appeared as a safe haven for my plans.
I'll fix the mooring cable to my prow from him,   770
once I have reached Athena's citadel.
And now I'll tell you all my plans:
attend my words, although they are not pleasant words to
    hear.
I'll send one of my servants asking Jason
to come and meet me face to face.   775
And when he's here, I'll reassure him with smooth words
and tell him I agree: that he is marrying well
the royal match he has contracted by betraying us°
and that this brings advantages, and is well planned.
And I'll request my children may stay here—   780
not that I wish to leave them in a hostile land
for enemies to foully treat my children°
no, but so that I can kill the princess by deception.
I'll send them carrying presents for her in their hands,
to take them to the bride so as not to have to leave this land:°   785
a finespun dress and plaited wreath of beaten gold.
If she accepts and puts the finery next to her skin,
she will die horribly, and so will anyone
who even comes in contact with the girl—
such are the poisons that I'll smear upon the gifts.
But now I'll leave that part of the story.   790
I grieve for the deed that I must do then:
that I must kill my sons—
there is no one can spirit them away.
And after I have utterly wrecked Jason's house,
I'll depart this land, escaping from the slaughter   795
of my beloved children, once I've steeled myself
to do this most abominable of deeds.
Because, my friends, to be derided
by one's enemies is not to be endured.
So let it be. What profit have I from my life?°

I have no fatherland, no home, no way to turn from my
    misfortunes.
My first mistake was when I deserted my ancestral home,   800
seduced by sweet talk from a man, a Greek—
with a god's help he will pay me dearly.
Nevermore shall he behold his sons from me alive;
nor shall he have a child with his new-wedded bride,   805
since she must die a horrid death by my strong poisons.
No one should think of me as slight and weak,
or as compliant—quite the contrary:
I'm deadly to my enemies, supportive to my friends.
It's people of this sort whose lives are crowned with glory.   810

CHORUS LEADER
Since you have shared this plan with us,
and since we'd like to help you, and promote the human law,
we tell you: do not do this thing.

MEDEA
There's no alternative.
It's understandable you talk like this
when you have not been made to suffer wrong like me.   815

CHORUS LEADER
But, woman, can you steel yourself to kill your body's fruit?

MEDEA
Yes, that's the way my husband can be deepest pierced.

CHORUS LEADER
You would become the wretchedest of women.

MEDEA
Then let it be. Meanwhile all words are mere excess.

(To a maid.)

You, go and summon Jason here   820
—you are the one I use for all my tasks of closest trust.
And tell him nothing of the things I have decided;

not if you are true to your mistress,
and if you are a woman born.

(Exit maid to the side; Medea stays on stage.)

CHORUS [*singing*]

STROPHE A

Through their forefather Erechtheus,
derived from gods by birth,   825
long have Athenians prospered,
bred from unconquered earth.
There they nourish their spirits
with arts famous and fine,
ever pacing with light steps   830
the luminous air's shine;
and the Muses, as they report,
the Pierian nine,
at one time gathered there to fill
fair Harmony with breath.

ANTISTROPHE A

And legend says that Aphrodite   835
scoops water with her hand
from the pure river Cephisus,
as all about the land
she blows breezes of sweet breath.
And ever plaiting round   840
a rose garland for her hair,
a sweetly scented crown,
she sends the pleasures of Desire
to sit beside wise Thought—   845
who work together to create
the best of every sort.

STROPHE B

This city of pure waters,
this land of friendly guidance,
how could it give asylum

to you, the children-killer?
hold you, impure, inside it?   850
Just think about the stabbing,
think of the actual murder.
Do not—they are your children—
we utterly implore you,
do not kill your own children.   855

Where can you find the will-power,°
where find the heart and vigor
to drive this gruesome daring?
Once you see your own darlings,
how can you then stay tearless,   860
as you stare at their slaughter?
No, you'll not have the power to,
not when they fall and beg you,
no, not to drench all gory
your hands, with heart remorseless.   865

(Enter Jason from the side.)

JASON

Well, here I am at your command.
Although you are so ill disposed, you should not be
deprived of this: I shall pay due attention. Woman,
what new is there that you might want from me?

MEDEA

Jason, I ask you to forgive the things I said.
It's only fair for you to tolerate   870
my angry moods, since there has been
much friendship between us in the past.
I came to words within myself, and scolded in these terms:
"Stubborn, why am I raging and resenting
those who show good foresight?
Why pit myself in conflict with the royal powers   875
of the land, and my own husband?

He's only taking the most advantageous course,
by marrying the princess, and producing siblings for my
　　sons.
So should I not relent from anger?
—what is wrong with me?—
the gods are taking helpful care of me.
I must confront the truth: that I have children,　　　　　880
and that we are exiles, much in need of friends."
And thinking through these things,
I recognized that I have been extremely stupid,
and mistakenly felt outraged.
So now I give approval; I believe you've shown good sense　　885
in forging this new kinship tie on our behalf—
it's I have been the fool.
I should have been there sharing in your plans,
advancing them: I should be waiting on your bed,
and gladly taking care of your new bride.
We . . . I do not say we're evil,
but we are just what we are . . . we women.　　　　　890
So you should not yourself
behave like us, and bandy trivial disputes.
I'm sorry, I admit I had it wrong back then;
but now I've thought things through more sensibly.
Children, my children, leave the house,
come here outside.

(The two boys and the Tutor come out from the house.)

Embrace your father, talk to him along with me,　　　　895
and with your mother now be reconciled from enmity
against those who should be near and dear.
We have made peace, and all our anger is dissolved.
Take his right hand.
Ah me! That makes me think of hidden wrongs.　　　　900
Will you live many years, my children,
to reach out your loving arms like this?

Poor fool, how close to tears I am, how racked by fear.
Here am I making up my quarrel with your father at long
  last,
and yet my tender sight's all blurring full of tears.   905

CHORUS LEADER
  A glistening tear has brimmed out from my eyes as well.
  I hope this present wrong may not advance yet further.

JASON   *overly confident*
  I like this thinking, and I don't blame those things,
  because it's only natural for females to be jealous,
  if some alien partner° gets imported to her bed.   910
  But now your feelings have been altered for the better,
  and you've recognized, eventually, the winning plan.
  These are the actions of a woman who is sensible.
  For you, my boys, your father has, with careful forethought,
  arranged, thanks to the gods, complete security.   915
  It's my belief that you, with your new brothers,
  shall enjoy the foremost standing in this land of Corinth.
  Your simple task is to grow up; the rest your father manages;
  and with some favorable god, I hope to see you thrive,
  and come to full maturity, superior to my enemies.   920

                                              (To Medea.)

  But you . . . why are your eyes engulfed with glistening tears?
  Why turn your pallid cheek away?
  Why not be glad to hear these words from me?

MEDEA
  It's nothing. I was only thinking of the children . . .   925

JASON
  Don't worry. I'll ensure that all goes well for them.

MEDEA
  I shall do as you say, and take your good advice.
  But woman is a tender creature and inclined to tears.°

JASON

But why on earth such grieving for the children here?

MEDEA

I gave them birth. And when you prayed
for life for them, a pang came over me   930
in fear for whether this would come to be.
But of the things you came to talk with me about:
some we have discussed, and there are others I have yet to
    mention.
Since the ruler has decided he will banish me,
I shall depart this land, an exile—
this is best for me, I know full well, and not to stay   935
and live where I might trouble you and the royal family,
since I'm considered hostile to this house.
But for the boys: if they're to be brought up by you,
you must beg Creon not to make them leave this land.   940

JASON

I'm not so sure I can persuade him, but I have to try.

MEDEA

At least then get your wife to beg her father
not to make the children leave this land in exile.

JASON

A good idea. And I believe I can persuade her—
if she is a woman like the rest of them.   945

MEDEA

I shall myself take part in this attempt as well:
I'll send her gifts, by far the most exquisite
known to humans of our times—
a finespun robe, and plaited wreath of beaten gold.°
And I'll have the children carry them.
One of you servants, bring the finery   950
out here as quickly as you can.

                    (She sends a maid into the house.)

She'll win good fortune in innumerable ways,
not only one: she'll get in you the best of husbands
as her bedmate, and acquire the finery   955
that Helios, my father's father,
handed down to his descendants.

(The maid enters from the house, bringing out to
Medea gifts which she hands to the two boys.)

Here, boys, take hold of these fine wedding gifts;
go and present them to the blessed royal bride.
She'll have no reason to complain at these.

JASON

You're being foolish: why deplete your own resources?
Do you believe the royal house is short
of dresses—short of gold, do you think?   960
Preserve these things; don't hand them out.
For if my wife holds me of any value, she'll estimate
my wish above material possessions, I am sure of that.

MEDEA

No, not your way. They say that gifts persuade the gods, even;
and gold means more to humans than a million words.   965
She has the divine touch; for now
the gods are raising her; she is the young empress.
And I would trade my life, not merely gold,
to get my boys reprieved from exile.
Now, boys, proceed inside the splendid palace,
and implore your father's newfound wife, my mistress;   970
beg her not to make you leave this land—
and give this finery to her. This is what matters most:
she must receive these gifts with her own hands.
Now quickly, off you go.
May you succeed and bring your mother
good reports about the things she longs to get.   975

(Exit the two boys to the side, with Jason and the Tutor.)

CHORUS [*singing*]

choral stasimon (handwritten annotation)

Now I've no hope for them, no longer,
the children cannot live, no longer;
they are already gone to slaughter.
The bride, unhappy girl, will take it,
the golden diadem, will take it;
and she shall set the crown of Hades   980
around her head—her hand will place it.

The charm and the unearthly glitter
will lure her to enfold around her
the robe and gold-entwined tiara.
She's dressing up to hold her wedding   985
down with the dead. Now she is heading
for such a trap, a fate so lethal,
she can't escape from disaster.

As for you, sad man, you've tied
a fatal knot with kings,   990
not knowing that it brings
the end of your boys' life,
and cruel death for your bride.
You were, unfortunate,
so wrong about your fate.   995

And I feel pain with you,
sad mother of the two,
you'll strike your children dead,
all for the marriage bed
your husband has betrayed—   1000
now he holds in your stead
another as his wife.

(*The Tutor and the two boys enter again from the side.*)

TUTOR

> Mistress, here are your sons, reprieved from banishment.
> Also the princess has received the wedding gifts
> delightedly with her own hands.
> So all's plain sailing for your boys in that direction.
> What's this?
> why rooted there confounded when you've done so well?   1005
> Why turn your pallid cheek away?°
> Why not be glad to hear these words from me?

MEDEA

> Ah me!

TUTOR

> This tune is not in harmony with my report.

MEDEA

> Ah me, again!

TUTOR

> Can I be bringing news
> of some misfortune I don't know about,
> mistaken in believing my report is good?   1010

MEDEA

> The news you've given is the news that you have given.
> I don't hold that against you.

TUTOR

> Then why cast down your eyes and shed these tears?

MEDEA

> There's no avoiding it, old man:
> the gods and I, with my bad thoughts,
> have engineered this outcome.

TUTOR

> Take comfort. You shall yet come back,   1015
> thanks to your children's influence.

[115] MEDEA

MEDEA

I shall myself fetch others back before that day,
to my own pain.

TUTOR

You're not the only woman to be sundered from her children.
You are a mortal, and must endure misfortunes.

MEDEA

Agreed. But go inside and make provision
for the children's daily needs.   1020

(Exit the Tutor into the house; the two boys stay on stage.)

O children, O my children,
you two have a city and a home,
and you shall leave me in my misery
to live for always there, cut off from your mother.
Meanwhile I'm heading for another country as an exile—
too soon to have enjoyed you, to have seen   1025
you happily grown up, too soon to decorate
your wedding bath, your wife, your marriage bed,
and raise up high the ceremonial torch—
unhappy in my willfulness.
For nothing, children, have I nurtured you,
for nothing gone through labor, and been raked with pain,   1030
enduring the sharp agonies of giving birth.
I used, poor fool, to pin all sorts of hopes on you:
that you would care for me when I was old,
and lay me out with your own hands when I was dead—
that's something people value highly.   1035
But now . . . this lovely kind of thought is finished now.
Deprived of you I shall drag through my bitter, painful days.
And you shall never see your mother more
with those dear eyes of yours, once you're transported
to another kind of life.
Ah, ah
why look at me like that, my little ones?   1040

why smile what is to be your latest smile of all?
Ah, ah,
what shall I do? My passion has all melted, women,
now that I see my children's shining looks.
I cannot, no.
Good-bye to all my former resolutions:
I shall convey my children from this land.   1045
Why should I use what's bad for them
to pierce their father's heart,
and so inflict upon myself double the pain as well?
No, I shall not. So good-bye, my resolutions.
But stop, what's wrong with me?
Do I want to be a laughing-stock,
and let my enemies get off scot-free?   1050
I must endure. It is mere cowardice
to even let such feeble words into my mind.
So, children, go inside.

to lose one's honor just cannot be endured

(The two boys stay on stage.)

Let anyone who thinks it wrong to stay
near to my sacrifice look after matters for themselves;   1055
I'll not unnerve my hand.
No, no, my heart, do not enact these things, I beg of you;°
just let them be, show mercy for the children.
They can live there with us, and bring you gladness.
No, by the avenging demons of the world below,
I swear, there is no way that I shall leave   1060
my boys among my enemies so they
can treat them with atrocity.
Now they are bound to die in any case, and since they must,
it will be me, the one who gave them birth,
who'll be the one to deal them death.
In any case these things are fixed and inescapable.
She has the garland on her head already;   1065
the princess-bride is in her death throes
in the gown, I'm sure of it.

But now, because I am about to tread
the most unhappy of all roads,
and I am sending these two down a track more wretched yet,
I want to say some parting words to them.
Come here, my children, reach out
your arms and hold your mother tight.   1070
O dearest arms, and dearest mouth,
and shapeliness, and children's noble looks!
May you fare well, but over there:
your father has despoiled what there is here.
Your lovely touch, your silken skin,
and such sweet children's breath!   1075
Away, go, go. I can no longer bear to look at you,
I'm overwhelmed by pain.
I realize what evil things I am about to do,
but it's my anger dominates my resolution—anger,
the cause of all the greatest troubles for humanity.   1080

(Exit the two boys into the house; Medea stays on stage.)

CHORUS [chanting]
Repeatedly I have explored
ideas of intricacy
and entered on deeper disputes
than usually womankind does.
We have inspiration as well   1085
that prompts dialogue leading truly
to wisdom (not everyone,
you'll only discover a few,
one woman among many more,
with true inspirational thought).

My conclusion is this: 1090
that people who've never had children,
and have no experience of them,
are certainly happier far

than those under parenthood's yoke.
With no opportunity to
experience children as joy,
nor as causes of pain—   1095
they steer clear of many ordeals.

And those with that sweetness of growth,
with children as plants in their house—
I notice how all of the time
they are worn down to shadows with cares.   1100
Struggling with how to nurture good health,
then how they can leave them well off . . .
and, after that, it's still unsure
just whether this labor is spent
to raise them as bad or as good.

And lastly I have to include   1105
one final disaster of all
for humans. Supposing all's well—
they've put aside plentiful means,
their children have grown to the full,
their character makeup is good—
still, if destiny has it this way,   1110
then Death takes their bodies below,
abducting your child's lovely life.
Yet how can it profit the gods
to pile upon humans this worst
and most agonizing of blows—   1115
a fine for the bearing of children.

MEDEA

I have been waiting for some time, my friends,
to see how things develop over there.
At last I see this man of Jason's coming;
his labored breathing shows he brings grave news.   1120

(Enter Servant from the side.)

SERVANT

Oh, you have done a terrible, atrocious crime,°
Medea. Run, run fast away—by sea-borne craft
or earth-borne chariot—take what you can.

MEDEA

And what has happened that demands escape like this?

SERVANT

They're dead—your poisons
have just destroyed the princess and her father Creon.   1125

MEDEA

That's excellent news—
I'll always number you among my friends and benefactors.

SERVANT

What's that? Can you be sane? Or are you mad?
To devastate the royal house, and then be pleased,   1130
and not afraid to hear of things like this?

MEDEA

I too have things I could reply.
But take your time, my friend, and tell me all:
how did they die? You'll give me twice
the pleasure if they met their end most horribly.   1135

SERVANT

When your two children and their father had arrived
inside the palace of the bride, we servants
who were anxious for your troubles were well pleased—
a lively rumor had just reached our ears
that you and your spouse had laid your former strife to rest.   1140
One of us kissed your children's hands, another kissed
their shining hair, and I myself accompanied
the youngsters to the women's chambers with a joyful heart.
The mistress we now wait upon instead of you,
before she saw your pair of boys,   1145
was glancing with excited looks toward Jason.

But then she covered up her eyes and turned away
her pallid cheek to show how much she loathed
the children's access there.
Your husband then set out to mollify
the woman's angry mood by saying this: 1150
"You should not be unfriendly to your own;
give up this anger and turn back your face.
Consider as your own, your dear ones, those your husband
    does.
Why not accept these presents, and entreat
your father to release the children from their banishment?—   1155
please, for my sake."
Once she had looked close at the finery, she was unable to
    resist;
she went along with everything her husband wanted.
And before he and your boys had gone
far from the palace, she unwrapped
the ornamented gown, and draped it round herself;
and placed the golden wreath about her curls;   1160
holding a burnished mirror to arrange her hair,
she smiled to see the lifeless image of her body there.
Then rising from her throne, she moved around the room,
stepping lightly on her snow-white feet.
She was enraptured by the gifts, and kept on looking down   1165
to check the dress was straight against her ankle.
But then there came a horrifying sight to see:
her color altered, and, with limbs convulsing,
she lunged sideways, collapsing on her throne,
and only just avoided falling on the floor.   1170
And some old serving woman, thinking that the fit
must be inspired by Pan, or through some god,
raised up the ritual glory cry—
until, that is, she saw white flecks of foam
discharging from her mouth,
her eyes contorting in their sockets,
her skin all drained of blood.   1175

Then she let out a piercing scream,
in answering discord to her earlier cry.
Immediately one maid set off toward
her father's chambers, and another to report
the bride's collapse to her new husband.
The building echoed through with hectic footsteps.   1180
After about the time that it would take a sprinting runner
to arrive at the finish of a two-hundred-meter racing track,
the wretched girl awakened from her silenced voice
and tight-shut eyes, and moaned a dreadful cry of pain.
Two pincer torments were invading her: 1185
first the golden band around her head spat
an astounding fountain of incendiary fire;
and then the clinging fabric, given by your boys,
began to eat into the poor girl's milky flesh.
Engulfed in flames she rose up from her throne,   1190
and bolted, shaking hair and head this way and that,
attempting to throw off the wreath.
But still the gold clung tightly by its fastenings;
and when she shook her hair,
instead the blazing doubled in intensity.
Then, overcome by agony,
she crumpled to the ground, unrecognizable   1195
to anyone except her parents' view.
The position of her eyes was not distinct,
nor any feature of her pretty face;
and blood was trickling from her crown, mixed sputtering
   with fire.
Her flesh was dripping from her bones like tears of resin,   1200
melted by the hidden action of your poison's jaws.
It was a fearsome sight, and all of us
were scared to touch her corpse—
forewarned by what had happened.
Her father, ignorant, poor man, of the disaster,
ran into the room and came upon her body.   1205
He cried aloud and flung his arms about her,

kissing her, and said: "O my poor child,
which of the gods has cut you down
so undeservedly like this? Which has bereaved me
of your life, an old man at death's door?
If only I could die with you, my child."   1210
When he had finished his lament,
and tried to stand his aged body back upright,
he found that, as with ivy gripping laurel branches,
he was held tightly by the finespun robe.
The struggle then was terrible.
While he did all he could to straighten up his limbs,   1215
she tugged him down again.
And if he tried to pull by force,
she wrenched the old man's flesh from off his bones.
And in the end he was exhausted and gave up the ghost,
poor man, no longer strong enough to fight the dreadful end.
And so they lie there corpses, daughter and old father, dead,° 1220
beside each other, a disaster that cries out for tears.
For me, your fate must lie beyond my scope;
you will discover for yourself
the payback of your punishment.
But as for human life, I think of it—
not for the first time—as a flitting shade.
I'm not afraid to say that those who seem to be so clever   1225
and who take such trouble over making speeches, those are
the very people who are guilty of the worst stupidity.
No human is a truly happy man:
it might be some are luckier than others
when prosperity flows with the tide . . .   1230
but truly happy—no.

(Exit Servant to the side.)

CHORUS LEADER
It would appear that on this day the god
is rightly loading many evils onto Jason's back.
O wretched daughter born of Creon, how much we pity you°

for your misfortunes. You've had to go away
to Hades' house, thanks to your union with Jason.   1235

MEDEA

My deed has been decided, friends—
as quickly as I can I'll end the children's lives,
and move on from this land.
I must make no delay, and give no time
for someone else's crueler hand to slaughter them.
Now they are bound to die in any case;   1240
and since they must, it will be me, who gave them birth,
who'll be the one to deal them death.
Come, come, my heart, it's time to put your armor on.
What use postponing now the evil deed,
inevitable acts that must be done?
Advance, my wretched hand, and grip the sword,
grip hard, and make toward life's painful finish line.   1245
No cowardice, and no remembering your children,
how they were your dears, or how you gave them birth.
Instead for this one fleeting day forget that they are yours,
and afterward take time to grieve.
Although it's you who's killing them,
they were your lovely babes.
And I'm a woman made of sorrow.   1250

(Exit Medea into the house.)

CHORUS [singing]

STROPHE A

I call on Earth and you, Sun, full
illumination,
look down and see this woman's foul
abomination,
before she strikes her deadly blow,
infanticidal.
Since they're descended from your glow,   1255
celestial, golden—

a fearsome thing for divine blood
in desecration
to fall to earth by human deed.
Fire transcendental,
great god of light, restrain, detain
her, exorcising
out from the house this deadly bane,
avenging demon.   1260

ANTISTROPHE A

In vain your toil for children, void,
evaporated;
in vain you bore the pair you loved,
obliterated,
you who escaped those narrow crags,
the most forbidding,
between the cobalt Clashing Rocks,
the never yielding.
Why does such heavy anger load   1265
you, soul-destroying?
Why does blood demand more blood?
For internecine
kin-murder brings for us humans
extreme pollution;
kin-killers bring down on their homes   1270
concordant anguish.

ONE BOY   *(Inside.)*

No! help, help!

CHORUS [*singing*]

STROPHE B

You hear the children? You hear their shout?°
O wretched woman, your cursed fate!

ONE BOY

What can I do to get free from my mother's grip?

THE OTHER BOY   (Inside.)
  I see no way, dear brother—we are lost.

CHORUS [singing]
  So should I enter? Yes, I choose   1275
  to fend off murder from these poor boys.

ONE BOY   (Inside.)
  Yes, for god's sake, help—now is our hour of need.

THE OTHER BOY   (Inside.)
  The net, the sword are closing in on us.

CHORUS [singing]
  So you are really made out of iron,   1280
  or out of granite. You will cut down
  the lives you nurtured from your womb's field,
  doom them to slaughter at your own hand.

                    ANTISTROPHE B
  I've heard of only one woman past,
  who killed the nurslings of her own nest.
  And that was Ino, sent mad by the gods,
  when Hera drove her wandering away from home.   1285
  She leapt down into the salty waves,
  wickedly drowning her clutch of babes.
  She pressed her steps from land into the sea,
  and died herself, along with her two sons.
  Can there be any event so foul   1290
  that it remains still impossible?
  The bed of women, love-bed of night—
  how many troubles are caused by your might.

              (Enter Jason from the side, alone and sword in hand.)

JASON
  You women standing by this building here,
  is the perpetrator of these dreadful things inside—Medea—

or has she run away in flight?   1295
She's going to have to hide herself deep underground,
or lift herself on wings high in the air above,
if she is to avoid due punishment from this royal dynasty.
Or does she think that she can kill the rulers,
and escape from this house here scot-free?   1300
But it's not her I came about:
much more my children.
Those that she has done damage to will do the same to her:
I've come to save the lives of my two sons,
and stop the kinsmen from inflicting harm
on them in retribution for the awful murder
that their mother has committed.   1305

CHORUS LEADER

O Jason, you unhappy man, you've no idea
how far you are advanced in troubles,
or you never would have said those words you did.

JASON

What's this? I don't suppose she wants to murder me as well?

CHORUS LEADER

Your boys are dead, dead by their mother's hand.

JASON

What are you saying, women? You have shattered me.   1310

CHORUS LEADER

Your children live no more—of that be sure.

JASON

Where did she kill them? Indoors, or outside the house?

CHORUS LEADER

Open the doors, and you will see your murdered sons.

(Jason tries to force open the doors.)

JASON

　　Quickly, undo the bars; quick, servants,
　　release the bolts, so I may see this double havoc　　　　　1315
　　both those who are dead, and her—so I may punish her.°

　　　　　　　　　　　(Medea appears above, in a flying chariot,
　　　　　　　　　　　　　　with the bodies of their two sons.)

MEDEA

　　Why rattle at these doors, and try to force them open?
　　Searching for the bodies
　　and for me the one who did it?
　　Then abandon all this effort.
　　And if you have some need of me,
　　then speak up if you wish.　　　　　　　　　　　　　　　1320
　　But you shall never lay your hands on me—
　　you see what kind of vehicle the Sun,
　　my father's father, has bestowed upon me,
　　as protection from unfriendly hands.

JASON

　　You thing of hate, woman most loathsome
　　to the gods, and me, and all humanity.
　　You who could steel yourself to drive your sword　　　　1325
　　into the children you yourself had borne;
　　and you have ruined me with childlessness.
　　Now you have done these things,
　　how can you dare to look upon the sun and earth,
　　when you've committed this abominable act?
　　To hell with you. Now I see straight: back then I was not
　　　　thinking,
　　when I conveyed you from your home　　　　　　　　　　1330
　　in a barbarian land to my household in Greece—
　　already then a powerful evil,
　　traitor to your father and the country that had nurtured you.
　　The gods have sprung on me the demon of revenge
　　that came with you, because you killed

your brother at the hearth, and then embarked
upon the *Argo*'s glorious deck.   1335
You started out from things like that;
and then, when you had married me
and borne my children, you murdered them—
all for the sake of sexual pride, the bed.
No woman born a Greek would ever have gone through
with such a crime; yet I saw fit to marry you,   1340
in preference to one of them—a loathsome
and destructive union it has proved to be for me.
A lioness not woman, you,
more cruel in nature than the Etruscan Scylla.
But not even with a thousand insults
could I pierce your skin, so toughened is your callousness;   1345
so go to hell, foul creature, and defiled with children's blood.
All I can do is grieve for my own destiny.
I never shall enjoy my new-laid marriage bed;
I never shall share words again
with these two children that I sowed and bred,
not in this life—no, they are lost to me.   1350

MEDEA
I might have contradicted you at length,
if it were not that father Zeus knows well
how you have fared by me,
and how you have behaved to me.
You can't have thought that you could spurn my marriage bed
and then proceed to live a life of pleasure,   1355
reveling in mockery of me?—
nor could the princess, nor could Creon who set up
this match, and wanted to eject me from this land,
and thought to get away with it.
So go ahead, and call me lioness
and Scylla, occupant of the Etruscan cave.°
I do not mind, since now I've fairly clawed into your heart.   1360

JASON

Yet you yourself must also suffer grief,
and be joint sharer in the sorrow.

MEDEA

Yes, surely, but the anguish is well worth it,
as long as you can't mock at me.

JASON

O my poor children, what a vicious mother
yours has proved to be.

MEDEA

O my poor boys, what a sad end you've met,
thanks to your father's failing.

JASON

It was not by my hand they died.   1365

MEDEA

It was, though, because of your own arrogance
and your new-saddled marriage.

JASON

And you believe it justified
to kill them for the sake of sex?

MEDEA

Do you suppose such troubles to be trivial for a woman?

JASON

It is for one who's sensible:
but everything is bad for you.

MEDEA

These children live no more, and that will pierce you
through.   1370

JASON

They are still here to bring down vengeance
on your guilt-stained head.

MEDEA

The gods know which one started this catastrophe.

JASON

For sure they know your mind and its full loathsomeness.

MEDEA

Yes, hate away.
The very timbre of your voice fills me with loathing.

JASON

And so does yours with me.
Our terms of parting will be easy.   1375

MEDEA

Then tell me—what am I to do?
I too am keen to bring this to an end.

JASON

Just let me bury and lament for these poor corpses.

MEDEA

Never—because I'll bury them with these my hands.
I'll take them to the shrine of Hera on the Peak
to make sure no one of my enemies   1380
can triumph over them by ripping up their graves.
I shall impose upon this land of Sisyphus
a solemn cult and festival for all of future time,
atonement for this heinous murder.
Then I shall make my way to Athens, country of Erechtheus,
where I shall cohabit with King Aegeus, son of Pandion.   1385
And you . . . you shall, appropriately enough,
meet a rotten end,
cracked on the head by a disintegrating piece
from off the *Argo*'s hulk,
and see the bitter outcome of your union with me.°

JASON [*chanting henceforth*]
*I pray that the children's Avenging Spirit
and Justice for murder may hound you to death.*   1390

MEDEA [*chanting henceforth*]
> What god or spirit is going to hear you,
> who perjured your oaths, and deceived your hosts?

JASON
> Child-killer, pollution!

MEDEA
> Back to your home and bury your wife.

JASON
> I go, bereft of both my sons. 1395

MEDEA
> It's early to lament: wait for your old age.

JASON
> My children, my darlings . . .

MEDEA
> Not your darlings—but their mother's!

JASON
> And that is why you murdered them?

MEDEA
> For you, to torture you with pain.

JASON
> I ache to enfold my sons,
> to touch their dearest lips! 1400

MEDEA
> Now you address them with love,
> now you desire to embrace,
> but then you pushed them away.

JASON
> Just allow me a touch
> of the delicate skin of my sons.

MEDEA

Unthinkable. Your words are wasted in air.

(*Medea flies away in the chariot with the bodies of their sons.*)

JASON

Pay attention to this, great Zeus: 1405
how I am driven away;
what I have suffered at the hands
of this polluted, this children-devouring she-lion.
With my every morsel of strength
I cry in my grief, and I call on the gods
to be witnesses,   1410
how you prevent me from touching
the children you killed,
deny me the burial rites for their bodies.
Would that I'd never begotten them,
only to see them lie butchered by you.

CHORUS [chanting]

Zeus stores many things on Olympus;°   1415
gods do many things that surprise us.
The endings expected do not come to pass:
those unexpected—the god finds a way.
That sort of story has happened today.

(*Exit all.*)

THE CHILDREN
OF HERACLES

Translated by MARK GRIFFITH

THE CHILDREN OF HERACLES: INTRODUCTION

The Play: Date and Composition

The date of *The Children of Heracles* (*Hêrakleidai, Heraclidae*) is uncertain. However, the metrical character of the verse is similar to that of *Medea* and Euripides' other early plays, suggesting that he most likely wrote the play in the late 430s or early 420s, perhaps ca. 430. It is not known with what other plays it was first staged nor how it fared in the dramatic competition that year.

On the basis of various apparent inconsistencies in the play (see below), some modern scholars have suggested that the version of it we have was revised in antiquity by someone other than Euripides, or that the text has suffered substantial damage in transmission. Moreover, five quotations that are attributed to this play by other ancient authors are not found in the text that has reached us via medieval manuscripts. The question of the integrity of the play as we have it remains open.

The Myth

After Heracles died (or became a god and was taken up to heaven), his son Hyllus and his other children were left without a stable home or male head of the family to protect them. Iolaus, who had been Heracles' comrade-in-arms in many of his labors, did his best to look after them, but they found themselves helpless against the continuing persecution of Eurystheus, king of Argos/ Mycenae. Eurystheus had also persecuted Heracles during his lifetime, and now he wished to eliminate all of Heracles' descendants. As Heracles' children fled from one city to the next all over Greece, Eurystheus threatened to attack each of the cities with

Argos' powerful army, and so none of them was willing to offer the children protection or a new home—except (in some versions, including this one) eventually Athens, which was ruled at the time by Theseus' two sons, Demophon and Acamas. In Euripides' play, we see how the Athenians successfully repelled the Argive attack, in part through the voluntary self-sacrifice of one of Heracles' daughters, and Eurystheus was captured and executed; so Heracles' children survived to found a future dynasty of "Dorian" rulers (the so-called Heraclids) in many regions of Greece. There are various oddities in Euripides' play as transmitted that have troubled scholars—for example, after the daughter of Heracles who offers to be sacrificed leaves the stage there is no further reference either to her or to her death, and at the end the chorus that so strongly opposed the killing of Eurystheus ends up simply agreeing to it.

The account of Athens' acceptance of the children of Heracles as suppliants is not attested before the fifth century BCE, when it is mentioned by various historians. It quickly became a symbol of Athenian pride and self-congratulation, and is often referred to by the Attic orators, especially in their speeches at commemorations of the Athenian soldiers who had fallen in combat. It may well have been invented in Athens as anti-Peloponnesian propaganda during Euripides' lifetime, though probably not by Euripides himself. The theme of Athens' acceptance of foreign suppliants and its military and religious protection of them against their enemies was very popular among fifth-century Athenian audiences. Some years later, Euripides himself treated an analogous legend in his *Suppliant Women* (written ca. 423 BCE); broadly similar episodes also serve as the basis for Euripides' lost *Erechtheus* (written about the same time as his *Suppliant Women*) and Sophocles' *Oedipus at Colonus*.

Iolaus (like Heracles) was a Theban hero, and it was part of Theban local legend that he was rejuvenated in Attica, the region containing Athens. So too, Euripides' account of the death of Eurystheus may have been based on tradition. On the other hand, the self-sacrifice of a maiden to save the rest of the group is a typically Euripidean motif and may well have been his invention. Other tragedies about the subject were apparently very rare. Aeschylus is known to have written a *Children of Heracles* but next to nothing is known about the play.

Transmission and Reception

The Children of Heracles has never been one of Euripides' most popular plays. It survived antiquity only by the accident of being among the so-called alphabetic plays (see "Introduction to Euripides," p. 3), and it is transmitted only by a single manuscript (and its copies) and is not accompanied by the ancient commentaries (scholia) that explain various kinds of interpretative difficulties. Further evidence that it was not very popular in antiquity is that no papyri bearing any parts of its text have been discovered. Two south Italian vases of the late fifth century BCE seem to illustrate the opening of *The Children of Heracles*; other ancient pictorial representations have also been assigned to this play by some modern scholars, but their attribution is very uncertain.

So too, the influence of the play on modern literature and art has been negligible, and only recently has the play begun to be adapted and performed.

THE CHILDREN
OF HERACLES

Characters   IOLAUS, friend and kinsman of Heracles
HERALD of Eurystheus, king of Argos
CHORUS of old men of Marathon
DEMOPHON, king of Athens
ACAMAS, his brother (silent character)
MAIDEN, daughter of Heracles
SERVANT of Heracles' son Hyllus
ALCMENE, mother of Heracles
MESSENGER
EURYSTHEUS, king of Argos

Scene: A temple of Zeus at Marathon, on the northeast coast of Attica. In front of the temple, an altar, at which old Iolaus and the young sons of Heracles have taken refuge as suppliants.

IOLAUS
Since long ago I've been convinced of this:
an honest man exists for those around him,
while the one whose mind is merely bent on profit
is useless to his city and dangerous to deal with,
good only to himself.
This I know from experience, not books.   5
I myself could have lived quietly in Argos,
but from concern and family duty I was
the one man who shared with Heracles
in his many labors, while he was still with us.
And now that he dwells in heaven, I keep his children

here under my wing and try to protect them—
though needing protection myself.   10
   For when their father left the earth behind,
Eurystheus hoped at first to kill us all:
but we escaped. So we have lost our city
but kept our lives. We wander now in exile,   15
fleeing from one town's boundaries to another's.
For, on top of our other miseries, Eurystheus
saw fit to inflict one further outrage on us:
whenever he heard we'd settled ourselves somewhere,
he sent heralds to demand we be extradited   20
and debarred from the land. He'd point out
that Argos was no small city, as friend or foe,
and that he himself was prosperous and successful.
And they, looking at the feebleness on my part
and at the children here, so small and without a father,
they ended up paying respect to the stronger power—
so everyone has barred us from their land.   25
For myself, I'm a fellow exile with the exiled children,
a fellow sufferer with these sufferers,
because I refuse to betray them, lest people might say,
"Look! Now that the children's father's not alive,
Iolaus has stopped protecting them,
even though he's a member of their family."   30
   With no place of our own in all of Greece,
we've come to Marathon and its neighboring lands;
we're sitting here, suppliants at the gods' altars,
asking for their help. For it is said
that Theseus' two sons live in this Attic plain;   35
of Pandion's descendants, they were the ones
to whom this land was allotted—
and they are related to these children here.
That is why we've come to the borders of famed Athens.
   Two agèd commanders have planned and led this flight: 40
the boys here are my concern, while Alcmene

is looking after her son's daughters inside the temple,
clasping them in her arms. We think it better
for young girls not to appear in public,
and to keep vigil instead at the altars.
Hyllus, and those of his brothers who are old enough,   45
are looking for some place on earth, a stronghold,
where we can settle if we're forced out from this land.

(The Herald enters from the side.)

Children, children, here, hold on to my robes!
I see Eurystheus' herald coming for us,
the one who pursues us, making us live as exiles,   50
depriving us of any place to rest.

(To the Herald.)

You scum, to hell with you and the man who sent you!
How many times did this same mouth of yours
deliver cruel messages to these boys' noble father!

HERALD

So you think the position you've taken up here's a good one,   55
and that you've come to a city which will be your ally—
but you're wrong. There's no one on earth who'll choose
your useless powers in preference to Eurystheus.
Get moving! Why trouble yourself like this?
You must pick yourself up and set off for Argos,
where the sentence of death by stoning awaits you.   60

IOLAUS

On the contrary, the god's altar will protect me
and this free country in which we have set foot.

HERALD

Do you want to make work for these hands of mine?

IOLAUS

Not by force will you drag me or them away with you.

HERALD

You will soon see.

(Seizing one of the children.)

You were not much of a prophet there, after all!   65

IOLAUS

As long as I live, this will not happen.

(They struggle; Iolaus is thrown to the ground.)

HERALD

Out of my way! However much you object,
I'm going to take them, since I think they belong to
    Eurystheus.

IOLAUS

All you who live in Athens, longtime residents,
help us! We're here as suppliants of Zeus,   70
the Guardian of the Meeting Place, and yet
we're being attacked and our garlands desecrated,
an insult to the city and an affront to the gods!

(Enter the Chorus from the side.)

CHORUS [*singing throughout their interchange with Iolaus and the
Herald, who speak in response*]
    Hey! What's this shouting, raised from near the altar?
    What mishap will it reveal to us? Quickly now!

STROPHE

    Look at that weak old man
    sprawled on the earth! Poor fellow!°   75

(To Iolaus.)

    Who is it that has thrown you so cruelly to the ground?

IOLAUS

    This is the one, strangers, who is dishonoring your gods
    by dragging me forcibly from the precinct of Zeus.

CHORUS

> *And you, old man, from what land have you come*　　　　80
> *to the people of the Four Towns? Was it from*
> *over the water, with oars, that you arrived here,*
> *leaving the shore of Euboea?*

IOLAUS

> It is no islander's life that I live, strangers:
> we've come here to your country from Mycenae.　　　　85

CHORUS

> *By what name did they call you, old man,*
> *the people of Mycenae?*

IOLAUS

> I'm sure you know of Heracles' companion,
> Iolaus. My deeds are not unheralded.

CHORUS

> *I do know, from hearing in time past. But, tell me,*　　　　90
> *whose are the young boys you are guarding in your arms?*

IOLAUS

> These are Heracles' children, strangers; they have come
> as suppliants to you and to your city.

CHORUS

> ANTISTROPHE
>
> *For what purpose? Please explain: are they anxious*　　　　95
> *to be allowed to speak with the city?*

IOLAUS

> They're anxious not to be extradited, or violently
> dragged from your gods and forced to go to Argos.

HERALD

> But this will in no way satisfy your masters,
> who've found you here and have you in their power.　　　　100

CHORUS

> *It is reasonable to respect the gods' suppliants, stranger,*

[145] THE CHILDREN OF HERACLES

and not to defile the seats of the deities with violent hands.°
Lady Justice will not be treated so.

HERALD

Just send these ones who belong to Eurystheus out   105
of the country, and I won't raise my hand in violence at all.

CHORUS

It's impious for a city to surrender
a suppliant group of strangers.

HERALD

But it is also good to keep one's foot out of trouble,
by adopting the more judicious alternative.°   110

. . . .

CHORUS LEADER

So, if you had any respect for a free country, shouldn't you
have spoken to the king of this land first, before
behaving so boldly and forcibly dragging the strangers
away from the gods' sanctuary?

HERALD

Who is the lord of this country and city?

CHORUS LEADER

The child of a noble father, Demophon, son of Theseus.   115

HERALD

Then the dispute about this case should be directed
to him: all else has been but wasted breath.

(Enter Demophon and Acamas from the side.)

CHORUS LEADER

But here he comes now in haste, together with
his brother Acamas, to hear these arguments.

DEMOPHON

Since, old as you are, you got here before us younger men,   120

in coming to the rescue here at Zeus' altar, tell us,
what's happening to bring together such a crowd? ⸱

CHORUS LEADER

These are the children of Heracles, my lord,
who, as you see, have put wreaths on the altar
and are sitting here as suppliants; and with them   125
is their father's trusty companion, Iolaus.

DEMOPHON

So why did this business have need for yelling?

CHORUS LEADER

That man there caused the shouting, by trying to take them
forcibly from the altar here; he knocked
the old man off his feet; we wept in pity to see it.

DEMOPHON

Well, his clothes and style are Greek, but these actions   130
are those of a barbarian.

(To the Herald.)

                              It's up to you
to tell me, then, and without wasting time,
what country's boundaries did you leave to come here?

HERALD

I am an Argive; that answers your question;
and I'm quite prepared to say for what, and from whom, I've
    come.   135
Eurystheus, king of Mycenae, has sent me here
to fetch these children. I came with ample justice
to my cause, stranger, both for words and actions.
    I am an Argive myself and I'm taking with me
these Argives, runaways from my own country,   140
who have been condemned to death by that land's decrees.
We who live in the city are entitled to pass

judgments on each other that are binding.
We've come to the hearths of many others too,
and taken our stand on these same arguments;   145
and none was so rash as to bring on himself new troubles.
But in you either they thought they saw some stupidity
and so came here, or else they're gambling
on a risk to get out of their desperate situation,
whether or not it will succeed.°   150
For they cannot expect that you in your right mind
will be the only person in all Greece
of all the places that they've visited,
to take pity on their hopeless predicament.

    Just weigh one alternative against the other: how
will you benefit from allowing them into your country,
or from letting us take them away? You stand to gain   155
from our side the great army of Argos and Eurystheus'
whole strength thus added to this city of yours.
But if you pay heed to their words and lamentations,
and grow soft, the affair turns into a spear contest;
for do not imagine that we'll give up this struggle   160
to recover them without recourse to steel.
Why then will you say that you're waging war on Argos?
What lands have you lost? Of what have you been robbed?
Who are the allies, what cause, in whose defense
you'll be burying the bodies of those men of yours who fall? 165
Bad will be your reputation with the citizens,
if, for the sake of an old man, at death's door,
a complete nothing, to put it in a word,
and of these children, you step deep into trouble.
At best, you can say just that you'll find some hope°—
and this far inferior to the present one.   170
For even fully grown and armed, these children
would hardly match the Argives (if that's what
now gives you heart and keeps your spirits high);
and long's the time in between, in which you all
may well be quite destroyed.

So do as I suggest:
by giving nothing, just allowing me   175
to take what's mine, win for yourself Mycenae.
That way you'll not suffer what you Athenians so often do;
that is, when you could choose stronger people
as friends, accepting weaker ones instead.

CHORUS LEADER
Who'd form a verdict, or decide a dispute, before
he's clearly heard the stories from both sides?   180

IOLAUS
My lord, since in your country this rule applies,
it is my right to speak and hear in turn,
and nobody will push me away first,
as they have done everywhere else.
Between this man and us there's nothing in common.°
Since, by decree, we are no longer part   185
of Argos, but are in exile from our country,
how could this man legitimately take us
as Mycenaeans, seeing that they themselves
expelled us from that land? So we are foreigners.
Or do you claim that anyone exiled from Argos   190
is exiled too from all Greek territories?
Well, not from Athens! Never in fear of Argos
will they drive Heracles' children from their land.
This is no Trachis, no Achaean city
from which, without justice but with impressive speeches
about Argos, like the ones you're giving now,   195
you'd drive out suppliants seated at the altar.
If that happens here, and they approve your arguments,
then no more shall I call their city "free."
But I know the Athenians' character, their nature:
they'll be prepared to die. Among good men   200
honor is regarded higher than staying alive.

                                        (To Demophon.)

Enough about the city; it brings resentment
to praise too strongly, as I know myself
from often being weighed down by too much praise.
But you personally are obliged, as I'll explain,   205
to protect these children, as leader of this country.
Pittheus was Pelops' son, then from Pittheus
came Aethra, and from her your father, Theseus.
Now their family tree I'll trace back over for you:
Heracles was son of Zeus and Alcmene,   210
and she was born from Pelops' daughter. So
your father and theirs are sons of first cousins.
So that is how your birth connection stands
to these children, Demophon; and I'll tell you too
what, apart from blood ties, you owe them. I can say   215
that once, when I was their father's right-hand man,
I was a fellow voyager with Theseus,
in pursuit of the Girdle that caused so much bloodshed.°
Later, it was Heracles who brought your father back
from out of the gloomy recesses of Hades.°
The whole of Greece is witness to those acts.
Now in return these children ask of you   220
this favor—that they not be extradited,
not be dragged from your gods and driven from this land.
So for you personally, it's a disgrace,
and likewise for the city, if suppliants,
wanderers, relatives—alas, just look at them, look!
are miserably dragged off from here by force.   225

　　I entreat you, as I wreathe you in my arms
and touch your beard: do not disdain to accept
the children of Heracles into your hands.
Be a true kinsman to them, a true friend,
father, brother—even master; any of these   230
is better than falling under the Argives' power.

CHORUS LEADER
　I pity them, my lord, when I hear their misfortunes.

Nobility defeated by bad luck—I see it here
in truth. These are children of a noble father,
and the fate they're suffering is surely undeserved.   235

DEMOPHON

A threefold path of circumstance° compels me,
Iolaus, not to reject these words of yours.°
The most important—Zeus, at whose altar
you sit with this, your flock of little fledglings.
Then there's the kinship and the debt I owe their father,   240
to treat them well for his sake. And finally
the disgrace to me, for which I must be most concerned:
for if I allow this altar to be robbed
violently, by a man from another land,
it will look as if I'm governing a country
that is not free, betraying these suppliants   245
out of fear of Argos. I'd rather hang myself!
Well, I could have wished you'd come with better fortune,
but even now, fear not: no one will drag
you or the children by force from this altar.

                                                    (To the Herald.)

As for you, return to Argos with this news   250
and tell Eurystheus also that if he
has some legitimate complaint against these strangers,
he'll obtain fair hearing. But you won't take them with you.

HERALD

Not even if it's just, and my claim is stronger?

DEMOPHON

How can it be just to take a suppliant by force?

HERALD

A disgrace to me, perhaps, but no harm to you!   255

DEMOPHON

It's my disgrace, if I let you drag them off.

HERALD

Just banish them from your borders: we'll take them from
there.

DEMOPHON

You're stupid if you think you know better than god.

HERALD

This is the place for the wicked to flee to, it seems.

DEMOPHON

The gods' sanctuaries are a common refuge for all.   260

HERALD

The Mycenaeans perhaps will not think so.

DEMOPHON

Am I not the one in charge of matters here?

HERALD

As long as you've got the sense not to injure them.

DEMOPHON

You can all be injured, so long as I don't defile the gods.

HERALD

I have no wish for you to have a war with Argos.   265

DEMOPHON

I'm of the same mind: but I'll not give these people up.

HERALD

But I'll take them none the less, since they're mine to take.

DEMOPHON

Then you will not find it easy to return to Argos.

HERALD

I'll try it out and see—immediately!

DEMOPHON

Then at once you'll be sorry that you laid hands on them.   270

HERALD

In the gods' name, don't you dare strike a herald!

DEMOPHON

I will, unless the herald learns how to conduct himself.

CHORUS LEADER   *(To the Herald.)*

Off with you!

                                                (To Demophon.)

And you, my lord, don't touch him!

HERALD

I'm on my way; one man's hands can put up
only a feeble fight. But I'll be back   275
with a mighty army of Argive spearmen, all
in Ares' bronze. Ten thousand warriors await me,
with King Eurystheus himself their commander;
he's waiting by the furthest boundaries
of Alcathous for the outcome of things here.
Brilliant and powerful, you will see him come,
descending upon you and your citizens,   280
this land and its crops, when he hears of your intransigence.
There'd be no point in having such great numbers
of fine young men in Argos, if we failed
to punish you.

DEMOPHON

To hell with you! I do not fear your Argos.
You were not going to come here, disgrace me,   285
and take these people away with you by force!
This city of mine's no vassal of Argos, but free.

                                        (Exit Herald to the side.)

CHORUS [*chanting*]

It is time to think, before Argive forces
reach the border. Keen is the war spirit
among the Mycenaeans, and keener still   290

will it be after this even than before.
For all heralds have the same habit
of exaggerating things to twice their size.
Can you imagine all he'll say to the king:
how terribly he was mistreated, and
how he barely escaped with his life?   295

IOLAUS

There's no finer treasure for children than
to have been born of a noble and good father
[and to take a wife from a noble family. I don't approve
of a man leaving disgrace for his children for the sake of
    pleasure,   300
if he gives in to desire and shares his bed with those beneath
    him].°
Good breeding resists ill luck better than ill breeding:
thus we, despite falling into the depths of adversity,
found these friends and relatives, who alone   305
of all the peoples of Greece stood up for us.
Children, offer them your right hands, yes, go ahead!

                                                (To the Chorus.)

And you, give your hands to the children, and draw near.

                            (The children and the Chorus clasp hands.)

Children, we have made proof of our true friends;
and if ever you find the chance to return   310
to your homeland, and occupy once more the house
of your father and recover his prerogatives,°
regard them as your friends and saviors, always;
and, in memory of this occasion, never raise
your spears in war against this land: regard it
as the most beloved and trusted city of all.   315
They deserve all due respect from you, since they
deflected from us and onto themselves instead

the hostility of such a mighty land
and its Pelasgian people; they could see
that we were wandering beggars, yet they didn't
surrender us or expel us from their country.
    For myself, sir, for as long as I shall live 320
I'll praise you to the heights, and when I die,
whenever that may be, in front of Theseus
I'll keep on praising you, gladdening his heart
by telling him how nobly you received
Heracles' children and protected them;
and how, true to your birth, you are maintaining
your father's glorious name all over Greece. 325
You were born of noble stock, but you are proving
to be in no way inferior to your father.
Of few others is this true: you could find perhaps
only one among many who's not worse than his father.

CHORUS LEADER

This country now and always has been ready
to help others in difficulties, if the cause is just. 330
And so it has undergone countless hardships
for the sake of friends, and I see here yet another
struggle approaching now.

DEMOPHON

You have spoken well, old sir, and I am sure
that things won't be different with these children here:
the favor will be remembered.
I now will bring together all the citizens 335
and marshal them in ranks, so we can meet
the Mycenaean army with full strength.
First I'll send out scouts in their direction,
lest they catch us unawares attacking suddenly
(for at Argos every man is swift in action).
Then I'll gather the seers, and we'll make the sacrifices. 340
As for you, please leave the altar here of Zeus

and go indoors with the children. There are people
who'll care for you, even if I am away.
Please go indoors, old sir.

IOLAUS

I will not leave the altar. We remain here,
sitting° as suppliants for the well-being of the city.   345
When you are safely delivered from this struggle,
then we'll go to a house.
The gods we have as allies aren't inferior,
my lord, to those of Argos. They are protected
by Hera, wife of Zeus, we by Athena;
and this I see as a basis for success,   350
that we in fact have better gods to help us,
for Pallas won't endure to be defeated.

(Exit Demophon and Acamas to the side.)

CHORUS [singing]

STROPHE A

Though you boast loud, others don't
care more about you,
stranger coming from Argos.   355
You will not frighten me with big words;
may that never happen
to great Athens and its fine choral dances.
You are out of your mind,   360
you and your king at Argos, Sthenelus' son!

ANTISTROPHE A

You have come to another city,
a city no inferior to Argos,
to drag off by force suppliants of the gods,
wanderers who've found sanctuary in my land;   365
this you do as a stranger, without deference
to kings, and presenting no alternative just claim.
Is this proper conduct
among men of good mind?

To me, peace is pleasing;   370
but to you, evil-minded king, I say this:
if you come against our city
you will not so easily obtain what you expect!
You are not the only one with lance   375
and bronze-covered shield of willow.
You shall never, for all your love of war,
throw this well-favored city into turmoil
with your spear; so hold back!   380

(Enter Demophon from the side.)

IOLAUS

Young man, why do you come with anxiety in your eyes?
Have you some news to tell about the enemy?
Are they waiting—or here already? What have you learned?
In any case, you won't prove false the herald's words.
Their commander, so successful in the past,   385
will come, I'm sure, with big thoughts in his mind
against Athens. But indeed Zeus is the punisher
of thoughts that are excessively ambitious.

DEMOPHON

They're here, the Argive force and King Eurystheus;
I saw them for myself—for the man who claims   390
to be an expert at commanding armies
should not use messengers to observe the enemy.
As yet, he has not launched his army here
into the plain, but he's stationed on the brow
of a rocky hill, and is spying out with care
(or so I guess—of course it's just opinion)   395
what best formation of troops he should employ°
to advance and get established in this land.
But my arrangements all are well completed:
the city's in arms, and sacrificial beasts
stand ready in their places to be slaughtered

for each one of the gods to whom they're due. 400
Burnt offerings conducted by the seers
fill all the city center, to ensure
rout of the enemy and safety for the city.°
And I've brought our oracle-singers all together
into one place, to make careful inquiry
into those ancient sayings, some published,
some secret, offering protection for this country.° 405
In most respects there are many differences
between the oracles; but there's one point
that stands out just the same in all of them:
they bid me slaughter, for Demeter's Daughter,
a young maiden born of noble father.

Myself, I've deep concern for your well-being, 410
as you can see; but I won't kill my own daughter,
nor will I compel any one of my citizens
to such an act against their will—and who
is so misguided as to hand over
willingly his own most precious children?
Even now you can see the bitter oppositions, 415
with people on one side saying I was right
to protect the suppliant strangers, while on the other
they denounce me as a fool. So if I do this now,
then civil war is already in the works.

So now you look, and see if you can help me 420
find some way for you all to be saved,
and this land too, without my having to fall
into conflict with my citizens.
My power's not absolute, as in barbarian nations;
but, if I act justly, I'll get justice in return.

CHORUS LEADER
Can it really be that though this city's eager 425
to help strangers in their need, god won't allow it?

IOLAUS
Children, we're just like sailors who have escaped

the fury of a storm and gained a grip
on land, but then are swept back out to sea
by fierce winds. So too we're now being driven   430
out from this land, just as we reached the shore
in seeming safety.
Ah!
Why ever did you cheer me so, cruel hope,
when you never intended to fulfill your promise?
This man's decision is understandable,   435
that he's not willing to kill his citizens' children.
And I can even accept what's happened here
without complaint: if it's the gods' decree
that I'm to fare like this, that is no reason
for my gratitude to you to disappear.
    Children, for you there's nothing I can do.
Where can we turn? Which god is still unwreathed,   440
which country's sheltering walls have we not visited?
We're done for, children; we'll surely be handed over.
As for myself, I don't care if I must die,
except that by dying I delight my enemies.
It's for you I weep and feel great pity, children,   445
and for your father's mother, old Alcmene—
how unfortunate you are in your long life!
(And I, too, wretched, enduring all for nothing!)
So after all it was fixed: we had to fall
into our enemy's hands, to end our lives
in shame and misery.   450

                                        (To Demophon.)

But you know how you can help? All hope's not gone
from my mind, of finding safety for these children:
give me to the Argives in their place, my lord,
and let them be saved without your facing danger.
Saving my life's irrelevant; let it go.   455
But what Eurystheus most would like to do
is capture me and so humiliate

Heracles' comrade. For the man is stupid.
Intelligent people certainly should wish
to find someone intelligent as their enemy,
not one thick and ignorant: greater is
the respect and justice they can expect to find.   460

CHORUS LEADER
Old sir, don't blame this city for what's happening.
Reproach against us may be made, we know,
untrue but no less nasty, that we betrayed
these strangers seeking our hospitality.

DEMOPHON   (To Iolaus.)
Your suggestion's noble, but unworkable.
It's not in search of you the king is marching
here with his army: what advantage is there   465
to Eurystheus if one old man dies? It's these,
the children, that he wants to kill, because
enemies are scared when noble sons are born
and young men remember their father's injuries:
that's what he must have foremost in his mind.   470
But if you have some other plan, more suitable,
then you propose it; myself, I'm at a loss
after hearing those oracles, and full of fear.

(Enter a Maiden from the temple.)

MAIDEN
Strangers, don't think my venturing outside
is in any way a sign of overboldness:
that is my first request of you.   475
For a woman, modest silence and reserve
are best, and staying quietly indoors.
But when I heard your groanings, Iolaus,
I came out, not as the appointed family head,
but, since I'm in some ways appropriate   480
for this, and also feel extreme concern

for these my brothers and sisters—and for myself—
I want to find out whether perhaps, on top
of all our previous troubles, now some new
and freshly added pain gnaws at your heart.

IOLAUS

My child, I have reason to praise you above all
of Heracles' children, and not only now.   485
Our family's fortunes,° which, it seemed, had made
good progress, now have fallen back again
into a hopeless state.
The king here says the singers of oracles
have signified that we must sacrifice
to Demeter's Daughter not a bull or heifer,
but a maiden girl, one who is noble-born,   490
if we are to survive and this city too.
So that's our hopeless state—because he says
that he himself won't slaughter his own children
nor anyone else's; and he's telling me
(not openly, but still it's what he means)
that, if we can't engineer a good solution,   495
we'll have to find ourselves some other country,
since his wish is to save this land from harm.

MAIDEN

Is this what holds us back from being saved?

IOLAUS

It is; in other respects we have been fortunate.

MAIDEN

Then fear no more the Argive's hostile spear!   500
I myself, old friend, without waiting to be told,
am ready to die, and to offer myself for slaughter.
For what are we to say, after the city
on our behalf agrees to face great danger,
if we ourselves just load our troubles off

onto others and, when we could save ourselves,°   505
we run in fear from death? No! it would be
ridiculous indeed for us to sit here wailing
as suppliants of the gods, and all this time,
sprung from that father from whom we are sprung,
to show ourselves as cowards. How can this   510
look right for honest people? I suppose
it's better to wait for this city to be captured
(which I pray may never happen!), and for me
to fall into our enemies' hands, and then,
after suffering great indignities and shame,
yes, me, the daughter of that noble father,
to end up seeing Hades just the same?
Or am I, driven from this land, to go   515
wandering elsewhere? Won't I be ashamed
if people say: "Why have you come here now
with suppliant branches, concerned only about your lives?
Get out of our land! We'll give no help to cowards."

    And again, even if my brothers and my sisters   520
were all to die, myself the sole survivor,
I'd have no prospect of a happy life
(though that's why many have betrayed their friends).
Who will want as wife a lone, deserted girl?
Who will want to have his children born from me?
Is it not better for me to die right now   525
than end up with this fate I don't deserve?
That other life might be more suitable
for a girl whose family's less renowned than mine.

    Lead me to where this body of mine must die,
wreathe me with garlands, begin the consecration,
if you are agreed°—
and conquer your foes! My life's here at your service,   530
ready and willing. I publicly proclaim:
for my brothers and sisters, and for myself, I die.
For, by choosing not to cling to life, I've found
the noblest prize: a death that's full of glory.

CHORUS LEADER

Ah! What can I say, as I hear this great speech   535
of a maiden who is ready thus to die
for her brothers and sisters? Who, of all mankind,
could speak or do things nobler than this girl?

IOLAUS

My child, you are indeed his, no one else's,
sprung from that hero and his immortal spirit,
true seed of Heracles. I feel no shame   540
at these your words, but pain at this misfortune.
But let me suggest how it can be done more fairly.
    We should summon all your sisters here, and then
we'll choose by lot the one who is to die
on behalf of the whole family: it's not right
for you to die without a lottery.   545

MAIDEN

I shall not die by a lottery's mere chance!
There is no favor in that; do not suggest it,
old friend. But, if you'll all accept my gift
and you're willing to make use of my eagerness,
I give my life for my brothers and my sisters   550
voluntarily, not under compulsion.

IOLAUS

Ah!
These words of yours are even more noble
than the previous ones—and those were fine indeed—
topping courage with courage, and speech with generous
    speech.   555
And yet, of course, I am not telling you,
nor yet forbidding you, to die, my child—
though by dying you do indeed benefit them all.

MAIDEN

What you say is sensible: you need not fear
a share in my pollution—I'll die freely.

Come with me, old friend; it's in your arms that I   560
would like to die; stand close by, cover over
my body with the robes. The slaughter's terror
is mine to face, and I am going now,
if I'm my father's daughter, as I claim.

IOLAUS

I couldn't bear to stand there at your death!

MAIDEN

Then ask the king here please to let me breathe   565
my life out, not in men's arms, but in women's.

DEMOPHON

It will be so, poor maiden. For you not
to be adorned with honor would disgrace me too—
for many reasons, but above all because
of your fearless heart and the justice on your side.
Of all the women that my eyes have seen   570
you are the most courageous. So now, if you wish,
to your brothers here say your final words
and to the old man, and then be on your way.

MAIDEN

Farewell, old friend, farewell! Please teach these boys
to be just like yourself, full of good sense   575
in everything—no more: that will suffice.
And keep on trying to keep them safe from death,
with all your heart; we really are your children,
and it is by your hands that we've been raised.
You see me now give up my own bridal day
to die in place of them. And you, my brothers   580
who're gathered here, may the gods bless you: may you
get those things for which my lifeblood's being shed!°
    Honor the old man, and the old lady inside there,
my father's mother, Alcmene, and these friends too.   585
And if one day release from suffering
is found for you by the gods, and final homecoming,

then remember how your savior should be buried—
with full splendor, as is deserved. I did not fail
in coming to your help, and I died for this whole family.   590
That, in place of children and maidenhood,
I possess as my treasure,° if there is anything in fact
to possess below the earth. And yet I pray
that there is nothing: for if we human beings
still have worries there when we are dead,
I don't know where to turn; for death's supposed
to be the greatest cure for miseries.   595

IOLAUS
But rest assured, you who of all women
stand out as greatest in courage: while you live,
you will be held by us in highest honor,
and so too after you have died. Farewell,
I shrink from uttering the wrong words   600
about the goddess to whom your body's dedicated,
Demeter's Daughter.

                    (Exit the Maiden and Demophon to the side.)

Children, I'm done for; my limbs give way in grief.
Take me and prop me against the altar here,
and cover me with this cloak. I take no pleasure
in all these doings; yet, if the oracle   605
is not fulfilled, life's over. That ruin
is more complete, but this one's bitter too.

CHORUS [singing]
                              STROPHE
No mortal man, I declare, is prosperous, or unlucky in his fate,
except through the gods:
and the same house does not stand firm for ever and ever   610
in good fortune;
different fates pursue it, one after another.
They reduce one man° from lofty to low estate,
And make the penniless wanderer° into a success.

It is not allowed to escape what is fated; nobody   615
can avert it by his brains,
and he who is eager to try
will forever face a futile task.

ANTISTROPHE

So, in your case—don't fall down from the blows of the gods, but
    bear up;
don't overtax your mind with grief.   620
Illustrious the portion of death that the wretched girl has,
death for the sake of brothers, sisters, and country;
not inglorious the fame that will greet her from humankind.
Virtue proceeds through struggle.
These actions are worthy of her father, and worthy   625
of her noble birth; and if you feel
due reverence for the deaths
of good people, I share this with you.

(Enter Servant from the side.)

SERVANT

Greetings, children! But where is the old man, Iolaus?   630
And your father's mother, is she far from this altar?

IOLAUS

We are present, all of us—at least if you can call me present.

SERVANT

Why are you lying there, with your eyes downcast?

IOLAUS

There's come a family worry, cause of distress.

SERVANT

Raise yourself now, keep your head up straight.   635

IOLAUS

I'm an old man; I have no strength in me.

SERVANT

Yet I have come here bringing you great joy.

IOLAUS

Who are you? Where have I met you? I don't remember.

SERVANT

I'm a serf of Hyllus: look, don't you recognize me?

IOLAUS

Dearest friend, you've really come to save us both?°   640

SERVANT

Yes; and what's more, you're assured of success in this.

IOLAUS

Mother of a noble son, Alcmene, I call you!
Come out and hear this man's most welcome news!
Long you've been wearing your life away in anxiety
about their return—and now they have arrived.   645

(Enter Alcmene from the temple.)

ALCMENE

Why is this whole building filled with shouting, Iolaus?
Surely it's not some herald here again
from Argos, aiming to manhandle you?
My own strength is weak indeed, stranger,
but this much at least you should know for certain:
there's no way that you will take them while I'm alive—   650
else may I no longer be known as Heracles' mother!
And if you lay a hand on them, you'll have
an ugly struggle with this aged pair.

IOLAUS

Take heart, old friend, and do not fear: no herald
has come from Argos bearing hostile words.   655

ALCMENE

Then why did you raise that shout, announcing fear?

IOLAUS

For you, so you'd come out in front of the temple.

ALCMENE

I do not understand. Who's this man here?

IOLAUS

He brings the message that your grandson's here.

ALCMENE

Greetings to you for this message! But why, if he   660
has set foot in this country, is he not
here now? Where is he? What circumstance has kept him
from appearing with you here to delight my heart?

SERVANT

He's positioning and marshaling the army that he brought.

ALCMENE

This discussion now no longer concerns me.   665

IOLAUS

It does concern you: but it is my job to inquire about it.

SERVANT

So what do you want to know of what has happened?

IOLAUS

How large a force of allies has he brought with him?

SERVANT

Many; beyond this I cannot tell the number.

IOLAUS

The Athenian leaders know of this, I suppose?   670

SERVANT

They know; and he's already stationed on their left wing.

IOLAUS

Then is the army now prepared for action?

SERVANT

Yes, and the sacrifices are ready near the ranks.

IOLAUS

So just how distant are the Argive spears?

SERVANT

Near enough that their commander can be clearly seen.   675

IOLAUS

Doing what? Is he marshaling the enemies' lines?

SERVANT

So we surmised; we couldn't actually hear.
But I'll go now; I shouldn't like my masters
to be without me when they clash with the enemy.

IOLAUS

And I'll go with you; for I naturally have   680
the same concern, to stand by my friends and help them.

SERVANT

It is most unlike you to say something so stupid.

IOLAUS

Unlike me too not to share with friends in battle.

SERVANT

Your strength, sir, is not what it used to be.°

IOLAUS

No enemy will withstand the sight of me.   685

SERVANT

No wound comes from a look, if the hand does nothing.

IOLAUS

What? Might not even I still pierce a shield?

SERVANT

You might, but first you'd be struck down yourself.

IOLAUS

But even so I'll be fighting° no smaller numbers.

SERVANT

Slight is the weight you add to your friends' side.   690

IOLAUS

Yet don't try to hold me back: I'm ready for action.

SERVANT

But you're not capable of action, only maybe of wishing for it.

IOLAUS

Say what you will, but still I shall not stop.

SERVANT

So how will you look as a soldier, without armor?

IOLAUS

Inside this building there are some captured weapons,   695
which I shall use. If I live, I shall return them;
and if I die, the god won't ask them back.
So go inside, take a suit of hoplite armor
down from the pegs, and bring it to me quickly.
It's a shameful housekeeping when some are fighting, but
     others   700
are staying behind because of cowardice.

                                   (*Exit the Servant into the temple.*)

CHORUS [*chanting*]
Time does not yet lay low your spirit;
it is still young and strong, but your body is gone to nothing.
Why do you struggle uselessly like this?
It will only hurt you and do little good for our city.   705
Old age should back down and give up on the impossible.
There's no way for you
to get your youthful strength back again!

ALCMENE

What's this? Are you out of your mind? Are you about
to leave me alone with my son's children?   710

IOLAUS

Battle is for men: your duty's to care for these children.

ALCMENE

What? If you die, then how shall I survive?

IOLAUS

Your son's sons—those who are left—will care for you.

ALCMENE

But what if (heaven forbid!) something happens to them?

IOLAUS

These friends here won't betray you; don't be afraid.   715

ALCMENE

That indeed is my hope; I don't have any other.

IOLAUS

Zeus too, I know, cares about your sufferings.

ALCMENE

Ah!
I won't be one to speak bad things of Zeus;
but only he himself knows if he is doing
his sacred duty toward me.

(Enter the Servant again from the temple.)

SERVANT

Here it is, as you see, the full suit of armor;   720
you've no time to lose in covering your body with it—
the battle is near, and Ares especially loathes
those who hang back. But if you fear the weight
of the arms, then walk ahead unclad for now,
and fit yourself out properly once you are
set in the ranks: I shall carry them until then.   725

IOLAUS

You are right. Please take the armor along for me

and keep it ready; put the ash spear in my hand,
and support my left arm as you guide my steps.

SERVANT

So the soldier needs to be tended like a child?

IOLAUS

My foot must be sure: it's a bad omen to slip or fall.   730

SERVANT

If only you were able to do all you're eager to do!

IOLAUS

Hurry! If I'm too late for the battle it will be terrible.

SERVANT

You're the slow one, not I, thinking you're doing something.

IOLAUS

Do you see my feet, how they're hurrying along?

SERVANT

I see you imagining more than really speeding.   735

IOLAUS

That's not what you'll say when you see me there . . .

SERVANT

Doing what? Enjoying success? I'd wish for that.

IOLAUS

Piercing one of our enemies right through his shield!

SERVANT

If we ever get there—that's my main concern.

IOLAUS

Ah!
O right arm of mine—if only you could be my ally now,   740
just as I remember you being in your prime,
back then when you captured Sparta, with Heracles!
What a total rout of Eurystheus I'd bring about—

he's a coward when it comes to facing the spear!
That's another thing wrong with great prosperity: 745
the appearance of courage. For we tend to think
that a man who's successful is good at everything.

(Exit Iolaus and Servant to the side.)

CHORUS [*singing*]

Earth and night-long Moon,
and most brilliant beams of the god who lights mankind, 750
carry the message for me!
Shout it out to heaven,
right up to the ruler's throne
and into the house of gray-eyed Athena:
I am ready, now that we've accepted these suppliants, 755
I am ready, for the land of my fathers and for our homes too,
to cut through danger with my gray steel.

Dreadful and strange it is
that a city like Mycenae, so fortunate and much praised 760
for its valor of spears,
hides a rage against my land.
But cowardly and low it would be,
O city of ours, to betray our
suppliant visitors at the orders of Argos. 765
Zeus is my ally; I feel no fear at all.
Zeus is just and he favors my undertaking. Never from my part
will gods be shown inferior to mortals.

Yet, O Lady Athena, 770
since yours is the soil of this land
and yours this city,
and you are its mother, its mistress, its protector,
send that man elsewhere, we pray,
who is leading unjustly this way the spear-force from Argos. 775

For my good will and good deeds, I do not deserve
to be cast out from house and home!

Always you receive from us
honors of multiple sacrifice,
a special day of the month,
never forgotten by us,
songs of young men and choral dances.   780
On the windy hillside
shrill cries of joy echo night-long,
with the rhythms of girls' feet beating.

(Enter a Messenger from the side.)

MESSENGER

Mistress, the report I bring is most beautiful
for you to hear, and short for me to tell:°   785
We've won! Victory trophies are being set up
bearing your enemies' captured weaponry.

ALCMENE

My dearest friend, to you this day's a blessing:°
for this report I hereby set you free!
But me—from one concern you've not yet freed me: 790
my fear, whether those I most want are still alive.

MESSENGER

They live—most glorious too in all the army.

ALCMENE

So the old one, Iolaus—he has survived?°

MESSENGER

Indeed—with god's help—he's done supremely well.

ALCMENE

You mean, he's accomplished some truly noble deed?   795

MESSENGER

He's young again, transformed from being old!

ALCMENE

You speak of a miracle! But first, describe the struggle,
the battle's happy outcome for our friends.

MESSENGER

A single speech from me will tell you all.
When all our troops were drawn up against theirs,   800
spearmen against spearmen, face to face,
Hyllus stepped down from his four-horse chariot
and stood there in the middle, between the lines.
Then he called out: "Commander, you have come
from Argos—but why can't we let this land°   805
of Attica be spared the pain of war?
Mycenae too, why harm your own fine city
by wasting its men's lives? Instead, with me
engage in single combat, one on one:
kill me, and take Heracles' children with you—
or die, and cede me my father's house and honors."   810
The army roared approval at his speech—
both their own release from toils, and his valor;
but he, Eurystheus, disregarding all those listeners
and unembarrassed by his own cowardice,
commander though he was, could not muster
the courage to approach the spears of war;   815
an abject coward, is that the man who came
to enslave the offspring of mighty Heracles?

  So Hyllus returned back into our own ranks;
and the seers, when they saw that single combat
was not about to bring us resolution,   820
without delay began the sacrifices,
cutting sheeps' throats to shed propitious blood.°
Then some stepped into chariots, while the infantry
lined up, their shields adjoining, side by side.
And then the Athenian king addressed his troops,   825
speaking exactly as a noble man should speak:
"My fellow citizens, now for the land that bore

and nurtured us, it's time to stand up strong!"
Meanwhile the other king was begging his allies
not to bring shame on Argos and Mycenae.

    The signal blared with Etruscan trumpet call,   830
and both sides joined in battle. Can you imagine
what clattering and clash of shields ensued,
what roars and groans of soldiers on all sides?
At first, the steady thrusts of Argive spears
broke up our ranks; but then they gave ground again.   835
The second phase: foot locked with foot,
man against man stood firm. The battle raged
and many fell. Commands were heard—just two:°
"Now listen, all of you whose home is Athens . . . ,"
"Listen, you who tend the soil of Argos . . . ,"
"Protect your city, fight off the shame of defeat!"   840
And finally, through toil and total effort,
we routed the Argive army, and they fled.
So then old Iolaus, seeing Hyllus
racing away, stretched out his right hand
and formally requested to mount his chariot;   845
he took the reins and urged the horses on
to overtake Eurystheus' chariot.

    Now, all I've said so far I saw myself,
but what comes next, I only heard from others.
As they passed by great Athena's sacred hill   850
in Pallene, he spied Eurystheus' chariot;
he made a prayer, to Hebe and to Zeus,
for just one day that he be young again,
so he could exact vengeance on his enemies.
What happened next is a miracle to hear about:
two stars settled above the horses' yoke
and cloaked the whole chariot in murky cloud—   855
your son and Hebe, the experts say these were.
And Iolaus out of this cloudy darkness,
showed forth young arms and body, strong again!
He captured the four-horse chariot of Eurystheus,

Iolaus did, in glory, by Sciron's cliff;   860
he bound his hands in chains; and now brings him
as finest first-fruit offerings for our victory,
their leader, once so prosperous and blessed!
He broadcasts by this present outcome, loud
and clear for all the world to hear, and learn:
we shouldn't envy those who seem to be   865
successful, 'til they're dead. Luck lasts one day.

CHORUS LEADER
Zeus, Lord of Victory, now for me it's possible
at last to see the daylight free from fear!

ALCMENE
Yes, Zeus: you were slow to notice all my troubles,
but now I thank you for the things you've done.   870
And my son—that he'd gone to live among the gods,
I doubted it before, but now I know it's true!
    Now, children, now you're freed from all your troubles,
free from accursed Eurystheus. So at last
you'll see your father's city, set your feet   875
on land you own by rightful inheritance,
make sacrifices to your ancestors' gods,
from whom you were kept away, as foreigners
wandering abroad in lives of utter misery.

(To the Messenger.)

But what was Iolaus' clever plan,
why did he spare Eurystheus and not kill him?   880
Please tell; for in my view it's not so clever
to capture your enemy but then not take full vengeance.

MESSENGER
It was for you, so that with your own eyes
you could see him grovel,° subjected to your hand.
Eurystheus did not want this, but by force his captor   885
made him comply: he'd rather not, alive,
come into your presence and pay his penalty.

Farewell, old lady; and be sure to remember
what you said first, as I began my report,
that you'd give me my freedom. In such matters   890
the nobly born should always keep their word.

CHORUS [*singing*]   (*Exit Messenger to the side.*)

STROPHE A

To me, dances are a delight,
and the clear-toned beauty of pipes at a feast;
a delight too is beautiful Aphrodite.
But especially pleasurable it is also   895
to see the good fortune of friends
who previously had not been expecting it.
Many indeed are the blessings
that generous Fate brings to birth,
and a human lifespan, child of Time.   900

ANTISTROPHE A

The road you are treading is just,
city of Athens; never should you give it up,
showing honor to the gods.
Anyone who contradicts this about you
is driving on the verge of craziness—
the proofs of this are being displayed here for all to see.   905
Conspicuous is the message that a god conveys,
ever taking from the proud
and thwarting their unjust plans.

STROPHE B

He is in heaven truly, old lady: 910
your son has indeed gone there.
It is proven, he did not go down
to the House of Hades
when his body was consumed by the dreadful flames.
He enjoys Hebe's lovely body now, his wife   915
in the golden hall of the gods.
Hymenaeus, god of marriage,
two children of Zeus you've thus most fitly honored!

Most people get what they are due.   920
To these children's father, they say
Athena was an ally; and now to them,
that same goddess' city and its people are their saviors,
checking the insolence of a man whose spirit
was violent and unlawful—until punished.   925
I pray that my mind
and my spirit never be so insatiable.

(Enter Servant from the side, accompanied by
soldiers leading captive Eurystheus.)

SERVANT

Mistress, you see—but I'll announce it anyway—
Eurystheus! Here he is, we've brought him to you,
a sight you barely hoped for, and for him
an outcome no less unimaginable.   930
He never dreamed he'd fall into your hands
when from Mycenae, with thick-massed ranks of shields,
he set out on his arrogant, unjust venture,
to capture and destroy this city, Athens.
But a god reversed things—the opposite occurred.   935
So Hyllus and noble Iolaus are at work
erecting a victory trophy, Zeus' icon.
To me they gave instructions, that I bring
this man to you. They want to warm your heart:
no pleasure's greater than to see one's enemy,
once fortunate, now ruined and brought low!   940

ALCMENE   (To Eurystheus.)
You're here, you scum? Justice has caught you at last?
So, first of all, turn your head toward me
and pluck up the nerve to look us in the eyes,
your enemies. You are in our power now,
you're no longer the boss.   945
Are you really that same man—I want to know this!—

the one who decided to torment my son when he
was alive (wherever he may be now), you villain,
by sending him off to kill hydras and lions?°
But about those evil tricks you planned, I'll say   950
no more. It would take too long to tell the story.
What outrage against him did you not attempt?
You even sent him—living—down to Hades.
But that was still not enough for you to dare:
me and the children, you kept on driving us
away, from all of Greece, though we were suppliants   955
of the gods, some of us old, others still just infants.

But you encountered men and a free city
that did not fear you. So you must die, abjectly;
and that's pure profit for you, dying just once
after inflicting so many torments on others.   960

SERVANT
It's not allowed for you to kill this man.

ALCMENE
If so, we captured him quite pointlessly;
but what's the law that keeps him now from dying?

SERVANT
This country's leaders think it isn't right.

ALCMENE
How so? They don't approve of killing enemies?   965

SERVANT
Not when they're caught in battle, still alive.

ALCMENE
So that's their view: did Hyllus just accept it?

SERVANT
You think he should reject this country's laws?

ALCMENE

I think Eurystheus should not go on living!

SERVANT

He should've died *then*; that was the first injustice!° 970

ALCMENE

Well, isn't it still right that he should pay?

SERVANT

There isn't anyone here who would kill him.

ALCMENE

I'm here—and I am someone, that's for sure!

SERVANT

You'll bear much censure if you do this act.

ALCMENE

I love this city—that can't be contradicted. 975
But since this man is finally in my grasp,
no one on earth shall ever take him from me.
That's that! If people want to call me bold,
a woman with thoughts too great for women's station,
let them say it! But this deed I will perform. 980

CHORUS LEADER

Terrible, and yet forgivable is the rage
that grips you against this man. Lady, I understand.

EURYSTHEUS

Lady, know well I shall not sweet-talk you:
I won't be saying things to save my life
for which I'd earn a charge of cowardice. 985
I did not start this feud of my own choice:
I knew I was your cousin born and bred,
and kin likewise to Heracles, your son.
But, like it or not, a divinity compelled me—
Hera, it was—to suffer this disease. 990
Then, once I'd taken up hostility

against him, and I recognized the challenge,
I grew to be an expert in torments,
spending my nights devising more, more ways
by which to keep at bay and kill my enemies,   995
and not forever share my life with fear.
I knew he was no cipher, but in truth
a valiant man, this son of yours, a hero.
Yes, enemy though he was, I speak well of him,
for he was noble.

    Then, after he'd departed, what was I to do?   1000
Hated by all his children here, aware
of this ancestral enmity, no stone I left
unturned, to kill, exile, manipulate:
by acting thus, I kept my interests safe.
But you, no doubt, faced with my situation,   1005
would never have expelled or treated badly
the resentful offspring of that lion, your enemy,
but kindly would have let them live in Argos?
A fine notion—but not to be believed!

    So, since they didn't execute me then
right on the spot, as I indeed desired,
now, by Greek law, to kill me is unholy.   1010
In sparing me, the city showed good sense,
respecting god much more than hating me.

    You've made your speech and heard me in reply;
and henceforth, since I'm hallowed° by the gods,
you have to call me "noble" evermore.   1015
So that is how things stand with me. To die
is not what I desire; and yet to leave
this life would not be burdensome at all.

CHORUS LEADER
    Alcmene, my advice to you is brief:
    release this man, as the city has decreed.

ALCMENE
    What if he dies, yet we obey the city?   1020

CHORUS

That'd be ideal—but how can it occur?

ALCMENE

I'll tell you, simply: after I've killed him
I'll give his body to his relatives
who come to fetch it. Thus toward his corpse
I'll not be violating any rules
made by the city. But this man will still
by dying pay his penalty to me.   1025

EURYSTHEUS   (To Alcmene.)

So, kill me! I do not beg you otherwise.
But since this city showed such reverence
and spared my life, I'll grant it now a gift,
an ancient oracle from Loxias:
great benefits it'll bring, more than you'd think.

                                              (To the Chorus.)

Once I'm dead, it's destined, you shall bury me   1030
at Pallene in front of Athena's temple,
the Maiden Goddess'. I shall lie there always
kindly both to you and to your city,
a savior and a resident underground.
But to the future descendants of these people
I'll be most hostile, if and when they come here
with a mighty army, betraying the good will   1035
and gratitude they owe you. (Such is the character
of these strangers you've defended as your guests!)
So why, you might ask, if I had learned all this,
did I still come here, and not stay at the shrine
respecting quietly° the oracle of the god?
I thought that Hera was more powerful
than oracles, by far, and she would not betray me.
Don't let them drip libations or blood offerings   1040
onto my tomb.°
In return for that, I'll make a grim return

for those invaders. Double will be your profit
from me in my death: your own great benefit
and the harm I'll do these Children of Heracles.

ALCMENE   *(To the Chorus.)*

So, why delay? If it's needed to bring salvation   1045
for the city and your descendants, kill him now,
since you've heard the words of this oracle.°
He's showing you a path completely safe.
The man's an enemy, and by his death
brings blessings and prosperity.

                                              (To the soldiers.)

Take him away, attendants, to that place   1050
and then after you've killed him give his body
to the dogs!°

                                              (To Eurystheus.)

And you—don't think you'll live to try again
to drive me out from my ancestral land!°

CHORUS [*chanting*]
This course seems best. Off you go, attendants;
for from our side of things
and for the royal family
all is and will be pure.

                                              (Exit all.)

HIPPOLYTUS

Translated by DAVID GRENE

HIPPOLYTUS: INTRODUCTION

The Play: Date and Composition

Euripides' *Hippolytus* was produced in Athens in 428 BCE. In the dramatic competition that year, Euripides took first prize, Iophon second, Ion third. It is not known what other three plays Euripides produced together with *Hippolytus*.

Ancient scholars report that this was the second play Euripides wrote about Hippolytus and Phaedra. They called this one *Hippolytus Bearing a Garland* (cf. lines 73ff. of the play) and the earlier one *Hippolytus Veiled*. The earlier version (its date is unknown) seems to have scandalized its audience by depicting Phaedra shamelessly yielding to her passion for Hippolytus and approaching the young man directly in order to seduce him; the title probably derived from his horrified reaction. Ancient authors cite about twenty small fragments or paraphrases from the earlier version and suggest that in the surviving version of the story Euripides "corrected . . . what was unseemly and worth condemning" in the earlier play; most modern scholars have followed their lead. If this is correct, it is the only case we know of in which an Athenian tragedian rewrote a play and staged the revised version in Athens. The ancient scholars also say that this tragedy is one of Euripides' best ones, and most readers, both ancient and modern, agree.

The Myth

Euripides' play begins with Aphrodite, the goddess of sexual desire, describing her resentment of Hippolytus, the son of the great Athenian hero Theseus by an Amazon, for his rejection of her and his devotion to Artemis instead. To punish Hippolytus, Aphrodite inflames Phaedra, Theseus' lawful wife, with an unwilling passion for her stepson. Phaedra attempts to suppress her desires and keep them secret, but her nurse conveys them to Hippolytus. When he reacts with horror and outrage, Phaedra fears that he will denounce her, and so she writes a letter accusing him of having raped her and then hangs herself. Theseus discovers her corpse and the letter, and in a rage he uses one of the three curses his father Poseidon had granted him to have Hippolytus killed.

Theseus was originally a hero associated with the small town of Troezen near Athens but was later incorporated into Athenian local mythology. Hippolytus likewise was worshipped in a cult in Troezen—girls who were about to marry sacrificed some of their hair to him—and also in Athens. There may well have been some links in myths and cult between Hippolytus and Aphrodite, since in both cases the sanctuary of Hippolytus also contained a temple of Aphrodite. Although there is no direct evidence for the story of Hippolytus, Phaedra, and Theseus before the fifth century BCE, it is likely to have been ancient even then. It is also worth noting that the basic plot pattern of the wife who fails to seduce her stepson and then accuses him of raping her (best known as the story of Potiphar's wife, from the biblical story of Joseph in the book of Genesis) seems to be part of the fundamental stock of folktales throughout the world and is found in different forms in many cultures and ages. In the fifth century BCE it was the subject not only of Euripides' two versions but also of a *Phaedra* by Sophocles of which very little is preserved (its date is also unknown, and there is no proof that it influenced or even preceded Euripides' second *Hippolytus*).

Transmission and Reception

Hippolytus was unusually successful when it was first produced—it supplied Euripides with one of the few victories he received in the dramatic competitions during his life—and it went on to become enormously popular and influential throughout antiquity and thereafter. As late as the second century CE, the travel writer Pausanias remarked that even barbarians who had learned the Greek language knew the story. It belongs to the group of ten plays by Euripides that were most widely diffused during ancient and medieval times. Its popularity among ancient readers is attested by eight papyrus fragments and clay sherds bearing small portions of texts of the play and dating from the third century BCE to the second century CE.

So it is not surprising that *Hippolytus* seems from our scanty evidence to have exerted considerable influence upon later Greek versions of the story, and it certainly influenced the two most important extant Roman versions: a poetic epistle from Phaedra to Hippolytus composed by Ovid in his *Heroides* and Seneca's tragedy *Phaedra*. In both of these, as in most of the later tradition (and perhaps already in Sophocles' lost *Phaedra*), the attention shifts markedly from Hippolytus to Phaedra. In the ancient visual arts, too, the story was extremely popular: in the fourth century BCE, south Italic vases depict Hippolytus' death; later, other artistic media, such as mosaics, paintings, sarcophagi, mirrors, coins, and gems, often depict Phaedra sitting sadly holding the letter and accompanied by the Nurse. Many Roman funerary sarcophagi represent on adjacent panels a whole sequence of episodes from the story, usually emphasizing Hippolytus hunting or dying, and often showing him with Phaedra or Theseus.

In modern times *Hippolytus* remains well known. Besides the frequent productions of Euripides' play on stages throughout the world in all languages (including ancient Greek), the story has offered material for numerous new versions. Jean Racine's *Phèdre* (1677) was only one of many dramatic versions of the story written in Renaissance France, but its genius has overshadowed them all—and has made Phaedra a classic figure of the modern stage. The challenge of turning Racine's French poetry into English verse has attracted numerous American and British poets, including Robert Lowell (1961), Richard Wilbur (1962), C. H. Sisson (1989), Derek Mahon (1999), and Ted Hughes (2000). At the end of the nineteenth century, Phaedra's passion inspired various poets (Algernon Charles Swinburne, *Phaedra*, 1866; Gabriele d'Annunzio, *Fedra*, 1908) and artists (Aubrey Beardsley, "Phèdre," 1898); and more recently it has especially drawn a number of women writers, such as H. D. (*Hippolytus Temporizes*, 1927), Marina Tsvetaeva (*Fedra*, 1928), Marguerite Yourcenar ("Phaedra, or Despair," 1936; *Who Doesn't Have His Minotaur?*, 1963), and Sarah Kane (*Phaedra's Love*, 1996).

Euripides' own play still appears on stages and in films, but less often than Racine's, and it continues to inspire modern dramatic versions, such as those by Eugene O'Neill (*Desire under the Elms*, 1924), Robinson Jeffers (*The Cretan Woman*, 1964), Tony Harrison (*Phaedra Britannica*, 1975), and Brian Friel (*Living Quarters*, 1977), as well as cinematic ones such as Jules Dassin's *Phaedra* (1962). Phaedra and to a lesser extent Hippolytus have also been the subject of a number of dance dramas (Martha Graham, *Phaedra*, 1962; *Phaedra's Dream*, 1983) and musical compositions (Christoph Willibald Gluck, *Ippolito*, 1745; Franz Schubert, "Hippolits Lied," 1826; Benjamin Britten, *Phaedra*, 1975), and have also been represented in several paintings (Peter Paul Rubens, ca. 1610; Théodore Géricault; Lawrence Alma-Tadema, 1860; Giorgio de Chirico, 1951ff.) and sculptures (J.-B. Lemoyne, 1715; Leonard Baskin, 1969).

HIPPOLYTUS 428 BCE

[handwritten annotations:]
Hippo exiled by theseus

she kills herself
↳ protects her reputation by leaving a note that Hippo raped her

○ won first prize
○ preceded by an earlier hippolytus

bastard son of Theseus

Characters THESEUS, king of Athens

HIPPOLYTUS, his son by the queen of the Amazons

PHAEDRA, Theseus' wife, stepmother to Hippolytus

A SERVANT

A MESSENGER°

THE NURSE

CHORUS OF WOMEN of Troezen

A CHORUS OF HUNTSMEN, in attendance on Hippolytus

APHRODITE

ARTEMIS

[handwritten annotations:]
Aphrodite causes her to fall in love with Hippo

arrogantly rejects the power of sexuality and desire

tells Hippo to have sex with Phaedra

gets sick bc she has overwhelming sexual desire for Hippo

Scene: Troezen, in front of the house of Theseus. In front of the house there are two statues, one of Artemis and one of Aphrodite.

(Enter Aphrodite.)

APHRODITE

[handwritten annotation: Aphrodite is upset because Hippolytus has dedicated himself too fully to virginity and the goddess Artemis]

I am called the Goddess Cypris:
I am mighty among men and they honor me by many names.
Of all who live and see the light of sun
from Atlas' pillars to the tide of Pontus,
those who worship my power in all humility
I exalt in honor.
But those whose pride is stiff-necked against me
I lay by the heels.

5

There is joy in the heart of a god also
when honored by men.
    Now I will quickly tell you the truth of this story.
Hippolytus, son of Theseus by the Amazon,   10
pupil of holy Pittheus,
alone among the folk of this land of Troezen has
    blasphemed me
counting me vilest of the gods in heaven.
He will none of the bed of love nor marriage,
but honors Apollo's sister, Artemis, Zeus' daughter,   15
counting her greatest of all divinities.
He is with her continually, this maiden goddess, in the
    greenwood.
He hunts with swift hounds and clears the land of wild beasts,
sharing in greater than mortal companionship.
I do not grudge him such privileges: why should I?   20
But for the wrongs that he has done to me
I shall punish Hippolytus this day.
I have no need to toil to win my end:
much of the task has been already done.
He came once from Pittheus' house to the country of Pandion
that he might see and be initiate in the holy mysteries.   25
Phaedra, his father's noble wife, saw him
and her heart was filled with the longings of dreadful love.
This was my work.
So before ever she came to this land of Troezen
close to the rock of Pallas that looks across to it,   30
she dedicated a temple to Cypris,
for her love dwells in a foreign land.
Ages to come will call this temple after him,
the temple of the Goddess Near Hippolytus.
When Theseus left the land of Cecrops,
flying from the guilty stain of the murder of the Pallantids,   35
condemning himself to a year's exile
he sailed with his wife to this land.
Here she groans in bitterness of heart

and the goads of love prick her cruelly,
and she is like to die—in silence,
and none of the servants know of her sickness.   40
But her love is not to end up that way.
I will reveal the matter to Theseus and all shall come out.
Father shall slay son with curses—
this son that is hateful to me.
For once lord Poseidon, the ruler of the sea,
granted this favor to Theseus,   45
that three of his prayers to the god would find answer.
Renowned shall Phaedra be in her death, but none the less
die she must.
Her suffering shall not weigh in the scale so much
that I should let my enemies go untouched
escaping payment of a retribution
sufficient to satisfy me.   50
    Look, here is the son of Theseus, Hippolytus!
He has just left the toils of his hunting.
I will leave this place.
See the great crowd of servants that throngs upon his heels
and sings the praise of Artemis in hymns!   55
He does not know
that the doors of death are open for him,
that he is looking on his last sun.

(*Exit Aphrodite. Enter Hippolytus from the side, attended by a
Chorus of friends and servants carrying hunting implements.*)

HIPPOLYTUS [*singing*]
*Follow me, follow me singing
of Artemis,
heavenly one, child of Zeus,
Artemis!
We are the wards of your care.*   60

CHORUS OF HUNTSMEN [*singing*]
Hail, mistress and queen, holiest one!

Hail, daughter of Zeus!
Hail, Artemis, maiden Daughter of Zeus and Leto!
Most beautiful of virgins by far!   65
Dweller in the spacious sky,
in the palace of your noble father,
in Zeus' golden glistening house!
Hail!
Maiden goddess most beautiful, most beautiful of all those who
    live in Olympus!   70

> (Hippolytus lays a garland on the statue of Artemis.)

HIPPOLYTUS
My sovereign lady, I bring you ready woven
this garland. It was I that plucked and wove it,
plucked it for you in your inviolate meadow.
No shepherd dares to feed his flock within it;   75
no reaper plies a busy scythe within it:
only the bees in springtime haunt the inviolate meadow.
Its gardener is the spirit Reverence who
refreshes it with water from the river.
Not those who by instruction have profited
to learn, but in whose very soul the seed   80
of purity and self-control toward
all things alike Nature has deeply rooted,
they alone may gather flowers there! The others,
the impure, may not.
    Loved Mistress, here I offer you this coronal;
it is a true worshipper's hand that gives it you
to crown the golden glory of your hair.
With no man else I share this privilege
that I am with you and to your words   85
can answer words. True, I may only hear:
I may not see you face to face.
So may I turn the post set at life's end
even as I began the race.

SERVANT

King—for I will not call you "Master," that belongs
to the gods only—will you take good advice?

HIPPOLYTUS

Certainly I will. I would not want to seem a fool.   90

SERVANT

In men's communities one rule holds good,
do you know it, King?

HIPPOLYTUS

                    Not I. What is this rule?

SERVANT

Men hate the haughty of heart who will not be
the friend of every man.

HIPPOLYTUS

                    And rightly too:
For a haughty heart breeds odium among men.

SERVANT

And affability wins favor, then?   95

HIPPOLYTUS

Abundant favor. Yes, and profit, too,
at little cost of inconvenience.

SERVANT

Do you think that it's the same among the gods?

HIPPOLYTUS

If we in our world and the gods in theirs
know the same usages—yes.

SERVANT

                    Then, King, how comes it
that for a venerable goddess you have not even
a word of salutation?

divine justice.
Artemis will kill Aphrodite
next (ave)

HIPPOLYTUS

          Which goddess?
Be careful, or you will find that tongue of yours   100
may make a serious mistake.

SERVANT

          This goddess here
who stands before your gates, the goddess Cypris.°

HIPPOLYTUS

I worship her—but from a long way off,
for I am pure.

SERVANT

          Yet she's a venerable goddess,
and great is her renown throughout the world.

HIPPOLYTUS

Men make their choice: one man honors one god,°
and one another.

SERVANT

          Well, good fortune guard you,
if you have as much good sense as you should have.   105

HIPPOLYTUS

A god of nocturnal prowess is not my god.

SERVANT

The honors of the gods you must not scant, my son.

HIPPOLYTUS

Go, men, into the house and look to supper.
A plentiful table is an excellent thing
after the hunt. And you

                        (Singling some out.)

rub down my horses.   110
When I have eaten I shall set them in the yoke and exercise
   them as is suitable.
As for your Cypris here—a long good-bye to her!

(Exit Hippolytus into the house accompanied by
the Chorus, except for the old Servant.)

SERVANT

O sovereign Cypris, we must not imitate
the young men when they have such thoughts as these.
As fits a slave to speak, here at your image   115
I pray and worship. You should be forgiving
when one that has a young tempestuous heart
speaks foolish words. Seem not to hear them.
You should be wiser than mortals, being gods.   120

(Exit the Servant. Enter Chorus of women of Troezen.)

CHORUS [singing]
STROPHE A
There is a rock streaming with water,
whose source, men say, is Ocean,
and it pours from the heart of its stone a spring
where pitchers may dip and be filled.
My friend was there and in the river water   125
she dipped and washed the royal purple robes,
and spread them on the rock's warm back
where the sunbeams played.
It was from her I heard at first
of the news of my mistress' sorrow.   130

ANTISTROPHE A
She lies on her bed within the house
and fever wracks her,
and she hides her golden head in finespun robes.
This is the third day   135
she has eaten no bread
and her body is pure and fasting.
For she would willingly bring her life to anchor
at the end of its voyage
in the gloomy harbor of death.   140

Is it Pan's frenzy that possesses you
or is Hecate's madness upon you, maid?
Can it be the holy Corybants,
or the Mighty Mother who rules the mountains?
Are you wasted in suffering thus   145
for a sin against Dictynna, queen of hunters?
Are you perhaps unhallowed, having offered
no sacrifice to her from taken victims?
For she goes through the waters of Limnae
and can travel on dry land beyond the sea,
the eddying salt sea.   150

Can it be that some other woman's love,
a secret love that hides itself from you,
has beguiled your husband,
the sovereign lord of Erechtheus'
people, that prince of noble birth?
Or has some sailor from the shores of Crete   155
put in at this harbor hospitable to sailors,
bearing a message for our queen,
and so because he told her some calamity
her spirit is bound in chains of grief
and she lies on her bed in sorrow?   160

Unhappy is the compound of woman's nature;
the torturing misery of helplessness,
the helplessness of childbirth and its madness,
are linked to it forever.
My body, too, has felt this thrill of pain,   165
and I called on Artemis, queen of the bow;
she has my reverence always
as she goes in the company of the gods.

[chanting]

But here is the old woman, the queen's nurse,   170
here at the door. She is bringing her mistress out.
There is a gathering cloud upon her face.
What is the matter? My soul is eager to know.
What can have made the queen so pale?
What can have wasted her body so?   175

(Enter the Nurse from the house, supporting Phaedra.)

NURSE [chanting, while Phaedra sings]
A weary thing is sickness and its pains!
What must I do now? What should I leave undone?
Here is light and air, the brightness of the sky.
I have brought out the couch on which you tossed
in fever—here, clear of the house.   180
Your every word has been to bring you out,
but when you're here, you hurry in again.
You find no constant pleasure anywhere
for when your joy is upon you, suddenly
you're foiled and cheated.
There's no content for you in what you have
for you're forever finding something dearer,
some other thing—because you have it not.   185
It's better to be sick than nurse the sick.
Sickness is single trouble for the sufferer:
but nursing means vexation of the mind,
and hard work for the hands besides.
The life of humankind is complete misery:
we find no resting place from calamity.   190
But something other dearer still than life°
the darkness hides and mist encompasses;
we are proved luckless lovers of this thing
that glitters in our world: no man
can tell us of that other life, expounding   195
what is under the earth: we know nothing of it.
Idly we drift, on idle stories carried.

PHAEDRA   (To the servants.)

Lift me up! Lift my head up! All the muscles
are slack and useless. Here, you, take my hands.
They're beautiful, my hands and arms!   200
Take away this headdress! It is too heavy to wear.
Take it away! Let my hair fall free on my shoulders.

NURSE

Quiet, child, quiet! Do not so restlessly
keep tossing to and fro! It's easier
to bear an illness if you have some patience   205
and the spirit of good breeding.
We all must suffer sometimes: we are mortal.

PHAEDRA

Oh,
if I could only draw from the dewy spring
a draught of fresh pure water!
If I could only lie beneath the poplars,   210
in the tufted meadow and find my rest there!

NURSE

Child, why do you rave so? There are others here.
Cease tossing out these wild demented words
whose driver is madness.

PHAEDRA

Bring me to the mountains! I will go to the mountains,   215
among the pine trees where the huntsmen's pack
trails spotted stags and hangs upon their heels.
By the gods, how I long to set the hounds on, shouting,
and poise the Thessalian javelin drawing it back—
here where my fair hair hangs above the ear—   220
I would hold in my hand a spear with a steel point.

NURSE

What ails you, child? What is this love of hunting,
and you a lady! Draught of fresh spring water?

Here, beside the tower there is a sloping ridge   225
with springs enough to satisfy your thirst.

PHAEDRA

Artemis, mistress of the Salty Lake,
mistress of the ring echoing to the racers' hoofs,
if only I could gallop your level stretches,   230
and break Venetian colts!

NURSE

This is sheer madness again,
that prompts such whirling, frenzied, senseless words.
Here at one moment you're afire with longing
to hunt wild beasts and you'd go to the hills,
and then again all your desire is horses,
horses on the sands beyond the reach of the breakers.   235
Indeed, it would need a mighty prophet, my child,
to tell which of the gods it is that
jerks you from your true course and thwarts your wits!

PHAEDRA [chanting]

O, I am miserable! What is this I've done?
Where have I strayed from the highway of good sense?   240
I was mad. It was the madness sent from some god
that made me fall.
I am unhappy, so unhappy! Nurse,
cover my face again. I am ashamed   245
of what I said. Cover me up. The tears
are flowing, and my face is turned to shame.
Having my mind straight is bitterness to my heart;
yet madness is terrible. It is better then
that I should die and know no more of anything.

NURSE [chanting]

There, now, you are covered up. But my own body: 250
when will death cover that? I have learned much
from my long life. The mixing bowl of friendship,

the love of one for the other, must be tempered.
Fondness must not touch the marrow of the soul. 255
Our affections must be breakable chains, that we
can cast them off or tighten them.
That one soul so for two should be in travail
as I for her, that is a heavy burden. 260
The ways of life that are most unbending
trip us up more, they say, than bring us joy.
They're enemies to health. So I praise less
the extreme than temperance in everything. 265
The wise will agree with me.

CHORUS LEADER
Old woman, you are Phaedra's faithful nurse.
We can see that the queen is in trouble, but the cause
that ails her is black mystery to us.
We would like to hear you tell us what is the matter. 270

NURSE [*speaking*]
I have asked and know no more. She will not tell me.

CHORUS LEADER
Not even what began it?

NURSE
                              And my answer
is still the same: of all this she will not speak.

CHORUS LEADER
But see how ill she is, and how her body
is wracked and wasted!

NURSE
                              Yes, she has eaten nothing
for two days now. 275

CHORUS LEADER
                              Is this the scourge of madness?
Or can it be . . . that dying is what she seeks?

NURSE

Dying? Well, she is starving herself to death.

CHORUS LEADER

I wonder that her husband allows this.

NURSE

She hides her troubles, says that she isn't sick.

CHORUS LEADER

But does he not look into her face and see   280
a witness that disproves her?

NURSE

                              No, he is gone.
He is away from home, in foreign lands.

CHORUS LEADER

Why, you must force her then, to find the cause
of this mind-wandering sickness!

NURSE

                              Every means
I have tried and still have won no foot of ground.
But I'll not give up trying, even now.   285
You are here and can in person bear me witness
that I am loyal to my masters always,
even in misfortune's hour.

    Dear child, let us both forget our former words.
Be kinder, you: unknit that ugly frown
and track of thought. And as for me, I'll leave   290
that point I could not follow you at: I'll take
another and a better argument.

    If you are sick and it is some unmentionable malady,
here are women standing at your side to help.
But if your troubles may be told to men,   295
speak, that a doctor may pronounce upon it.
So, not a word! Oh, why will you not speak?
There is no remedy in silence, child.

Either I am wrong and then you should correct me;
or right, and you should yield to what I say.
Say something! Look at me!   300
   Women, I have tried and tried and all for nothing.
We are as far as ever from our goal.
It was the same before—she was not melted
by anything I said, and now she still won't listen.
   But this you shall know, though to my reasoning
you are more dumbly obstinate than the sea:
If you die, you will be a traitor to your children.   305
They will never know their share in a father's palace.
No, by the Amazon queen, the mighty rider
who bore a master for your children,
one bastard in birth but trueborn son in mind,
you know him well—Hippolytus . . .

PHAEDRA
   Ah!

NURSE
   So that has touched you?   310

PHAEDRA
   You have killed me, nurse. For the gods' sake, I entreat you,
   never again speak about that man to me.

NURSE
   You see? You have come to your senses, yet despite that,
   you will not make your children happy nor
   save your own life besides.

PHAEDRA
   I love my children.
   It's another storm of fortune that batters me.   315

NURSE
   There is no stain of blood upon your hands?

PHAEDRA

My hands are clean: the stain is in my heart.

NURSE

The hurt comes from outside? Some enemy?

PHAEDRA

One I love destroys me. Neither of us wills it.

NURSE

Has Theseus done some wrong against you then?   320

PHAEDRA

May I be equally guiltless in his sight!

NURSE

What is this terror urging you to death?

PHAEDRA

Leave me to do wrong. My wrongs are not against you.

NURSE

Not of my will, but yours, you'll cast me off.

PHAEDRA

Are you trying to force me, clasping my hand as suppliant?   325

NURSE

Your knees too—and I never will let you go.

PHAEDRA

Sorrow, nurse, sorrow for you, if you find out.

NURSE

Can I know greater sorrow than losing you?

PHAEDRA

It will kill you. But for me, honor lies in silence.

NURSE

And yet you hide it, though I plead for what's good?   330

PHAEDRA

Yes, for I seek to win good out of shame.

NURSE

But won't you earn more honor if you speak?

PHAEDRA

By the gods, let go my hand and go away!

NURSE

No, for you have not given me what you must.

PHAEDRA

I yield. Your suppliant hand compels my reverence.   335

NURSE

I will say no more. Yours is the word from now.

PHAEDRA

Unhappy mother, what a love was yours!

NURSE

It is her love for the bull you mean, dear child?

PHAEDRA

Unhappy sister, bride of Dionysus!

NURSE

Why these ill-boding words about your kin?   340

PHAEDRA

And I the unlucky third, see how I end!

NURSE

Your words are wounds. Where will your tale conclude?

PHAEDRA

Mine is an inherited curse. It is not new.

NURSE

I have not yet heard what I most want to know.

PHAEDRA

Ah!

If you could say for me what I must say myself. 345

NURSE

I am no prophet to know your hidden secrets.

PHAEDRA

What does it mean to say someone's in love?

NURSE

Sweetest and bitterest, both in one, at once.

PHAEDRA

One of those two, I've known, and all too well.

NURSE

Are you in love, my child? And who is he? 350

PHAEDRA

There is a man . . . his mother was an Amazon . . .

NURSE

You mean Hippolytus?

PHAEDRA

You

have spoken it, not I.

NURSE

What do you mean? This is my death.
Women, this is past bearing. I'll not bear
life after this. A curse upon the daylight!
A curse upon this shining sun above us! 355
I'll throw myself from a cliff, throw myself headlong!
I'll be rid of life somehow, I'll die somehow!
Farewell to all of you! This is the end for me.

   Chaste and temperate people—not of their own will—
fall in love, badly. Cypris, you are no god.

You are something stronger than a god if that can be.   360
You have ruined her and me and all this house.

                                        (*Exit the Nurse.*)

CHORUS [*singing*]
                    STROPHE
Did you hear, did you hear
the queen crying aloud,
telling of a calamity
which no ear should hear?
I would rather die
than think such thoughts as yours.   365
I am sorry for your trouble.
Alas for troubles, man-besetting.
You are dead, you yourself
have dragged your ruin to the light.
What can happen now in the long
dragging stretch of the rest of your days?
Some new thing will befall the house.   370
We know now, we know now
how your love will end,
poor unhappy Cretan girl!

PHAEDRA
Hear me, you women of Troezen who live
in this extremity of land, this anteroom to Argos.
Many a time in night's long empty spaces   375
I have pondered on the causes of a life's shipwreck.
I think that our lives are worse than the mind's quality
would warrant. There are many who know good sense.
But look. We know the good, we see it clear.   380
But we can't bring it to achievement. Some
are betrayed by their own laziness, and others
value some other pleasure above virtue.
There are so many pleasures in this life—
long gossiping talks and leisure, that sweet curse.

Then there is shame that thwarts us. Shame is of two kinds.   385
The one is harmless, but the other's a plague.
For clarity's sake, we should not talk of "shame,"
a single word for two quite different things.
These then are my views. Nothing can now seduce me   390
to the opposite opinion. I will tell you
in my own case the track which my mind followed.
    At first when love had struck me, I reflected
how best to bear it. Silence was my first plan:
to conceal that illness. For I knew the tongue
is not to be trusted: it can criticize   395
another's faulty thoughts, but on its owner
it brings a thousand troubles.
    Next, I believed that I could conquer love,
conquer it with discretion and good sense.
And when that too failed me, I resolved to die.   400
And death is the best plan. No one will dispute that.
I want to have my virtues known and honored—
not many witnesses when I do something wrong!
I know what is involved: I know the scandal;   405
and all too well I know that I am a woman,
object of hate to all. Destruction light
upon the wife who first did shame her bed
by dalliance with strangers. In the wives   410
of noble houses first this taint began:
when wickedness approves itself to those
of noble birth, it will surely be approved
by their inferiors. Truly, too, I hate
lip-worshippers of purity and temperance, who
own lecherous daring when they have privacy.
O Cypris, sea-born goddess, how can they   415
look frankly in the faces of their husbands
and never shiver with fear lest their accomplice,
the darkness and the rafters of the house,
take voice and cry aloud?
This then, my friends, is my destruction:

I cannot bear that I should be discovered   420
a traitor to my husband and my children.
God grant them rich and glorious life in Athens—
famous Athens—freedom in word and deed,
and from their mother an honorable name.
It makes the stoutest-hearted man a slave
if in his soul he knows his parents' shame.   425
The proverb runs: "There is one thing alone
that stands comparison with life in value,
a quiet conscience,"...a just and quiet conscience
for whoever can attain it.
Time holds a mirror, as for a young girl,
and sometimes as occasion falls, it shows us
the evildoers of the world. I would not wish
that I should be seen among them.   430

CHORUS LEADER
  How virtue is held lovely everywhere,
  and harvests a good name among mankind!

                              (*Enter the Nurse again.*)

NURSE
  Mistress, the trouble you told me just now,
  coming on me so suddenly, frightened me;
  but now I realize that I was foolish.   435
  In this world second thoughts, it seems, are best.
  Your case is not so extraordinary,
  beyond thought or reason. The goddess in her anger
  has smitten you, and you are in love. What wonder
  is this? There are many thousands suffer with you.
  So, you will die for love? And all the others,   440
  who love, and who will love, must they die, too?
  How will that profit them? The tide of Cypris,
  at its full surge, is not withstandable.
  Upon the yielding spirit she comes gently,

but if she finds one arrogant and superior   445
she seizes him and abuses him completely.
Cypris wings her way through the air; she is in the sea,
in its foaming billows; from her everything
that is, is born. For she engenders us
and sows the seed of desire whereof we're born,   450
all we her children, living on the earth.
He who has read the writings of the ancients
and has spent much time with poetry, knows well
that Zeus once loved the lovely Semele;
he knows that Dawn, the bright light of the world,
once ravished Cephalus hence to the gods' company   455
for love's sake. Yet they still dwell in heaven
and do not flee in exile from the gods—
they are content, I am sure, to be subdued
by the stroke of love.
But you, you won't submit? Why, you should certainly
have had your father beget you on fixed terms   460
or with other gods for masters, if you don't like
the laws that rule this world. Tell me, how many
men of good enough sense do you suppose
turn a blind eye to the sickness of their marriage;
how many fathers have helped their erring sons
procure a lover? It is the wise man's part   465
to leave in darkness everything that is ugly.
    We should not in the conduct of our lives
be too exacting. Look, see this roof here—
these overarching beams that span your house—
could builders with all their skill lay them dead straight?
You've fallen into the great sea of love
and with your puny swimming would escape!   470
If in the sum you have more good than bad,
count yourself fortunate—for you are mortal.
    Come on, dear child, give up your wicked thoughts.
Give up your insolence. It's only insolent pride

to wish to be superior to the gods.   475
Endure your love. A god has willed it so.
Indeed, you are sick. So try to find some means
to turn your sickness into health again.
There are magic love charms, spells of enchantment;
we'll find some remedy for your lovesickness.
Men would take long to hunt devices out,   480
if we the women did not find them first.

CHORUS LEADER

Phaedra, indeed she speaks more usefully
for this present trouble. But it is you I praise.
And yet my praise brings with it more discomfort
than do her words: it is bitterer to the ear.   485

PHAEDRA

This is the deadly thing that devastates
well-ordered cities and the homes of men—
this art of all-too-attractive-sounding words.
It's not the words ringing delight in the ear
that one should speak, but those that have the power
to save their hearer's honorable name.

NURSE

This is high moralizing! What you need   490
is not fine words, but the man! Come, let's be done,
and tell your story frankly and directly.
For if there were not such danger to your life,
or if you were a pure and temperate woman,
I never would have led you on so far,   495
merely to please your fancy or your lust.
But now a great prize hangs on our endeavors,
and that's the saving of a life—yours, Phaedra!
There's none can blame us for our actions now.

PHAEDRA

What you say is wicked, wicked! Hold your tongue!
I will not hear such shameful words again.

NURSE

Oh, they are shameful! But for you they're better   500
than noble-sounding moral sentiments.
The deed is better if it saves your life
than your good name in which you die exulting.

PHAEDRA

For the gods' sake, do not proceed any further!
What you say sounds good, but is terrible!
My very soul is subdued by my love
and if you plead the cause of wrong so well   505
I'll fall into the ruin that now I flee.

NURSE

If that is what you think, ideally, you'd be virtuous;
But if not, you should obey me: that's next best.
It has just come to my mind, I have in the house   510
some magic love charms. They will end your trouble;
they'll neither harm your honor nor your mind.
They'll end your trouble . . . only you must be brave.
But first we need from him you desire some token—
a lock of his hair or some piece of his clothes—
we'll take this and make one joy out of two.   515

PHAEDRA

This charm: is it an ointment or a drink?

NURSE

I don't know. Don't be overanxious, child,
to find out what it is. Accept its benefits.

PHAEDRA

I fear you will be too clever for my good.

NURSE

You are afraid of everything. What is it you fear?

PHAEDRA

You surely will not tell this to Theseus' son?   520

NURSE

Come, let that be: I will arrange all well.
Only, my lady Cypris of the Sea,
be my helper you. The other thoughts I have
I'll tell to those we love within the house;
that will suffice.

(Exit the Nurse into the house.)

CHORUS [singing]

STROPHE A

Eros, Eros that distills desire upon the eyes,   525
that brings bewitching grace into the heart
of those you would destroy:
I pray that you may never come to me
with murderous intent,
in rhythms measureless and wild.
Not fire nor stars have stronger bolts   530
than those of Aphrodite sent
by the hand of Eros, Zeus's child.

ANTISTROPHE A

In vain, in vain by Alpheus' stream,   535
in the halls of Phoebus' Pythian shrine
the land of Greece increases sacrifice.
But Eros the king of men we honor not,   540
although he keeps the keys
of the temple of desire,
although he goes destroying through the world,
author of dread calamities
and ruin when he enters human hearts.

STROPHE B

The untamed Oechalian filly who had never known   545
the bed of love, known neither man nor marriage,
the goddess Cypris gave her to Heracles.
She took her from the home of Eurytus,

maiden unhappy in her marriage song,
wild as a Naiad or a Bacchant,   550
with blood and fire, a murderous wedding song!

ANTISTROPHE B

O holy walls of Thebes and Dirce's fountain   555
bear witness you, to Cypris' grim journeying:
once you saw her bring Semele to bed,
lull her to sleep, clasped in the arms of Death,
pregnant with Dionysus by the thunder king.   560
Love is like a flitting bee in the world's garden,
and for its flowers destruction is in its breath.

PHAEDRA   (Listening at the door.)
Women, be silent!
Oh, I am destroyed forever.   565

CHORUS LEADER
What is there terrible within the house?

PHAEDRA
Hush, let me hear the voices within!

CHORUS LEADER
And I obey. But this is sorrow's prelude.

PHAEDRA
Oh no!
Oh, I am the most miserable of women!   570

CHORUS [singing, while Phaedra speaks]
What does she mean by her cries?
Why does she scream?
Tell us the fear-winged word, mistress,
rushing upon the heart.

PHAEDRA
I am lost. Go, women, stand and listen there yourselves   575
and hear the tumult that falls on the house.

CHORUS

Mistress, you stand at the door.
It is you who can tell us best
what happens within the house.
Tell me, tell me, what evil has befallen.   580

PHAEDRA

It is the son of the horse-loving Amazon,
Hippolytus, cursing my servant maid.

CHORUS

My ears can catch a sound,   585
but I can hear nothing clear.
I can only hear a voice that has come,
that has come through the door.

PHAEDRA

It is plain enough. He cries aloud against
the mischievous bawd who betrays her master's bed.   590

CHORUS

Lady, you are betrayed!
How can I help you?
What was hidden is revealed.
You are destroyed.
Those you love have betrayed you.   595

PHAEDRA

She loved me and she told him of my troubles,
and so has ruined me. She was my doctor,
but her cure has made my illness fatal now.

CHORUS LEADER

What will you do? There is no cure any more.

PHAEDRA

I know of one, and only one—quick death.
That is the only cure for my disease.   600

(Enter Hippolytus and the Nurse from the house.)°

HIPPOLYTUS

O Mother Earth! O Sun and open sky!
What words I have heard from this accursed tongue!

NURSE

Hush, son! Someone may hear you shouting.

HIPPOLYTUS

You cannot expect that I'll hear horror in silence!

NURSE

I beg you, by your strong right hand, don't speak!   605

HIPPOLYTUS

Don't lay your hand on me! Let go my cloak!

NURSE

By your knees then . . . don't destroy me!

HIPPOLYTUS

                              What is this?
Don't you declare that you have done nothing wrong?

NURSE

Yes, but the story, son, is not for everyone.

HIPPOLYTUS

Why not? A pleasant tale makes pleasanter telling,
when there are many listeners.   610

NURSE

You will not break your oath to me, surely you will not?

HIPPOLYTUS

My tongue swore, but my mind was quite unpledged.

NURSE

Son, what would you do? You'll not destroy your friends?

HIPPOLYTUS

"Friends"!
I spit the word away. None of the wicked
are friends of mine.

NURSE

                        Then pardon, son. It's natural
that we should make mistakes, since we are human.   615

HIPPOLYTUS

Women! This coin which men find counterfeit!
Why, why, Lord Zeus, did you put them in the world,
in the light of the sun? If you were so determined
to breed the race of man, the source of it
should not have been women. Men might have dedicated
in your own temples images of gold,   620
iron, or weight of bronze, and thus have bought
the seed of progeny ... to each been given
his worth in sons according to the assessment
of his gift's value. So we might have lived
in houses free of the taint of women's presence.
But now, to bring this plague into our houses   625
we destroy° the fortunes of our homes. In this
we have a proof how great a curse is woman.
For the father who begets her, rears her up,
must add a dowry gift to pack her off
to another's house and thus be rid of the load.
And he again that takes the cursed creature   630
rejoices and enriches his heart's jewel
with dear adornment, beauty heaped on vileness.
With lovely clothes the poor wretch tricks her out
spending the wealth that underprops his house.
For of necessity either one weds well,°
rejoicing in his in-laws, but must keep   635
a bitter bed; or else his marriage works
but his in-laws are useless, so that benefit
is all he has to counteract misfortune.

That husband has the easiest life whose wife
is a mere nothingness, a simple fool,
uselessly sitting by the fireside. 640
I hate a clever woman—yes, I pray
that I may never have a wife at home
with more than woman's wits! Lust breeds mischief
in the clever ones. The limits of their minds
deny the stupid ones lecherous delights.
We should not suffer servants to approach them, 645
but give them as companions voiceless beasts,
dumb—but with teeth, that they might not converse,
and hear another voice in answer.
But now at home the mistress plots the mischief,
and the maid carries it abroad.
                  So you, vile woman, 650
came here to me to bargain and to traffic
in the sanctity of my father's marriage bed.
I'll go to a running stream and pour its waters
into my ear to purge away the filth.
Shall I who cannot even hear such impurity,
and feel myself untouched—shall I turn wicked? 655
Woman, know this. It is my piety saves you.
Had you not caught me off guard and bound
my lips with an oath, by heaven I would not refrain
from telling this to my father.
Now I will go and leave this house until
Theseus returns from his foreign wanderings,
and I'll be silent. But I'll watch you close. 660
I'll walk with my father step by step and see
how you look at him . . . you and your mistress both.
I have tasted of the daring of your infamy.
I'll know it for the future.° Curses on you!
I'll hate you women, hate and hate and hate you,
and never have enough of hating . . .
                    Some
say that I talk of this eternally, 665

yes, but eternal, too, is woman's wickedness.
Either let someone teach them to be temperate,
or allow me to trample on them forever.

(Exit Hippolytus to the side.)

PHAEDRA° [*singing*]

ANTISTROPHE

Bitter indeed is woman's destiny!
I have failed. What trick is there now, what cunning plea   670
to loose the knot around my neck?
I have had justice. Oh, earth and the sunlight!
Where shall I escape from my fate?
How shall I hide my trouble, dear friends?
What God or man would appear
to bear hand or part in my crime?   675
There is a limit to all suffering and I have reached it.
I am the unhappiest of women.

NURSE°

Alas, mistress, all is over now.   680
your servant's schemes have failed and you are ruined.

PHAEDRA

This is fine service you have rendered me,
corrupted, damned seducer of your friends!
May Zeus, the father of my father's line,
blot you out utterly, raze you from the world
with thunderbolts! Did I not see your purpose,   685
did I not say to you, "Breathe not a word of this"
which now overwhelms me with shame? But you,
you did not hold back. And so it's without honor
that I will die.
Enough of this. We need a new scheme now.
The anger of Hippolytus is whetted.
He will tell his father all the wrongs you did,   690
to my disparagement. He will tell old Pittheus, too.
He will fill all the land with my dishonor.

May my curse
light upon you, on you and all the others
who eagerly help unwilling friends to ruin.

NURSE

Mistress, you may well blame my ill success,   695
for sorrow's bite is master of your judgment.
But I have an answer to make if you will listen.
I reared you up. I am your loyal servant.
I sought a remedy for your love's sickness,
and found . . . not what I sought.
Had I succeeded, I'd have been a wise one.   700
Our wisdom varies in proportion to
our failure or achievement.

PHAEDRA

                                      So, that's enough
for me? Do I have justice if you deal me
my deathblow and then say "I was wrong: I grant it"?

NURSE

We talk too long. True, I was not wise then.
But even from this desperate plight, my child,   705
you can escape.

PHAEDRA

                                      You, speak no more to me.
You gave me then dishonorable advice.
And what you tried has brought dishonor too.
Away with you!
Think of yourself. For me and my concerns
I will arrange all well.

                    (Exit Nurse into the house.)

You noble ladies of Troezen, grant me this,   710
this one request, that what you have heard here
you wrap in silence.

CHORUS LEADER

I swear by holy Artemis, child of Zeus,
never to bring your troubles to the daylight.

PHAEDRA

I thank you. I have found one sole device   715
in this unhappy business, one alone,
so that I can pass on to my children after me
life with an uncontaminated name,
and myself profit by the present throw
of Fortune's dice. For I will never shame you,
my Cretan home, nor will I go to face   720
Theseus, defendant on an ugly charge,
never—for one life's sake.

CHORUS LEADER

What is the desperate deed you mean to do,
the deed past cure?

PHAEDRA

                            To die. But the way of it, that
is what I now must plan.

CHORUS LEADER

                            Oh, do not speak of it!

PHAEDRA

No, I'll not speak of it. But on this day
when I shake off the burden of this life   725
I shall delight the goddess who destroys me,
the goddess Cypris.
Bitter will have been the love that conquers me,
but in my death I shall at least bring sorrow
upon another, too, that his high heart
may know no arrogant joy at my life's shipwreck;
he will have his share in this my mortal sickness   730
and learn to be more temperate himself.

CHORUS [*singing*]

STROPHE A

Would that I were under the cliffs, in the secret hiding places of
    the rocks,
that a god might change me to a wingèd bird
and set me among the feathered flocks.
I would rise and fly to where the sea   735
washes the Adriatic coast,
and to the waters of Eridanus.
Into that deep-blue tide,
where their father, the Sun, goes down,
the unhappy maidens weep
tears from their amber-gleaming eyes   740
in pity for Phaethon.

ANTISTROPHE A

I would win my way to the coast,
apple-bearing Hesperian coast,
of which the minstrels sing,
where the lord of the ocean
denies the voyager further sailing,   745
and fixes the solemn limit of heaven
which giant Atlas upholds.
There the streams flow with ambrosia
by Zeus's bed of love,
and holy Earth the giver of life,   750
yields to the gods rich blessedness.

STROPHE B

O Cretan ship with the white sails,
from a happy home you brought her,
my mistress over the tossing foam, over the salty sea   755
to bless her with a marriage unblessed.
Black was the omen that sped her here,

black was the omen for both her lands,
for glorious Athens and her Cretan home,
as they bound to Munychia's beach   760
the cables' ends with their twisted strands
and stepped ashore on the continent.

ANTISTROPHE B

The presage of the omen was true;   765
Aphrodite has broken her spirit
with the terrible sickness of impious love.
The waves of destruction are over her head,
from the roof of her room with its marriage bed,
she will tie the twisted noose.   770
And it will go around her fair white neck!
She felt shame at her cruel fate.
She has chosen good name rather than life:
she is easing her heart of its bitter load of love.   775

NURSE   (*Within.*)

Ho, there, help!
You who are near the palace, help!
My mistress, Theseus' wife, has hanged herself.

CHORUS LEADER

It is done, she is hanged in the dangling rope.
Our queen is dead.

NURSE   (*Within.*)

Quick! Someone bring a knife!   780
Help me cut the knot around her neck.

(*Individual members of the Chorus speak.*)

FIRST WOMAN

What shall we do, friends? Shall we cross the threshold,
and take the queen from the grip of the tight-drawn cords?

SECOND WOMAN

Why should we? There are servants enough within

for that. Where outsiders intervene,
there is no safety.   785

NURSE   *(Within.)*
Lay her out straight, poor lady.
Bitter shall my lord find this housekeeping.

THIRD WOMAN
From what I hear, the queen is dead.
They are already laying out the corpse.

(Theseus enters from the side.)

THESEUS
Women, what is this crying in the house?   790
I heard heavy wailing on the wind,
as it were servants, mourning. And my house
deigns me, a returning envoy, no warm welcome.
The doors are shut against me. Can it be
something has happened to my father? He is old.   795
His life has traveled a great journey,
but bitter would be his passing from our house.

CHORUS LEADER
Theseus, it's not the old that trouble has struck.
Young is the dead one, and bitterly you'll grieve.

THESEUS
My children . . . has death snatched a life away?

CHORUS LEADER
Your children live—but sorrowfully, King.   800
Their mother is dead.

THESEUS
                        It cannot be true, it cannot.
My wife! How could she be dead?

CHORUS LEADER
She herself tied a rope around her neck.

THESEUS

Was it grief and numbing loneliness drove her to it,
or has some misadventure been at work?

CHORUS LEADER

I know no more than this. I, too, came lately
to mourn for you and yours, King Theseus.   805

THESEUS

Oh,
why did I plait this coronal of leaves,
and crown my head with garlands, I the envoy
who find my journey end in misery?
Servants! Open the doors! Unbar the fastenings,
that I may see this bitter sight, my wife
who killed me in her own death.   810

(The door is opened, revealing Phaedra's corpse.)

CHORUS [*in the following exchange, the Chorus sings, the Chorus Leader
speaks, and Theseus sings the lines in italics and speaks the others*]
Woman unhappy, tortured,
your suffering, your death,
has shaken this house to its foundations.
You were daring, you who died
in violence and guilt.
Here was a wrestling: your own hand against your life.   815
Who can have cast a shadow on your life?

THESEUS

STROPHE

Bitterness of sorrow!
Extremest sorrow that a man can suffer!
Fate, you have ground me and my house to dust,
fate in the form of some ineffable
pollution, some grim spirit of revenge.   820
The file has whittled away my life until
it is a life no more.

I am like a swimmer that falls into a great sea:
I cannot cross this towering wave I see before me.   825
My wife! I cannot think
of anything said or done to drive you to this horrible death.
You are like a bird that has vanished out of my hand.
You have made a quick leap out of my arms
into the land of Death.
It must be the sin of one of my ancestors in the dim past   830
gods in their vengeance make me pay now.

CHORUS LEADER

You are not the only one, King.
Many another as well as you
has lost a noble wife.   835

THESEUS

ANTISTROPHE

Darkness beneath the earth, darkness beneath the earth!
How good to lie there and be dead,
now that I have lost you, my dearest companion.
Your death is no less mine.   840
Where did this deadly misfortune come from,
poor woman, upon your heart?
Will any of you
tell me what happened?
Or does the palace keep a flock of you for nothing?
Oh,° the pain I saw in the house!
I cannot speak of it, I cannot bear it. I am a dead man.   845
My house is empty and my children orphaned.
You have left them, left them, you
my darling wife—
the best of wives   850
of all the sun looks down on or the blazing stars of the night.

CHORUS

Woe for the house! Such storms of ill assail it.
My eyes are wells of tears and overrun,
and still I fear the evil that shall come.   855

THESEUS

But wait a moment!
What is this tablet fastened to her dear hand?
Does it want to tell me some news?
Has the poor woman written begging me to care
for our marriage and children?
Sad one, rest confident.   860
There is no woman in the world who shall come to this house
and sleep by my side.
Look, the familiar golden signet ring,
hers who was once my wife, beckons me!
Come, I will break the seals,
and see what this letter wants to tell me.   865

CHORUS

Surely some god
brings sorrow upon sorrow in succession.°
The house of our lords is destroyed: it is no more.   870

CHORUS LEADER

God, if it so may be, hear my prayer.°
Do not destroy this house utterly. I am a prophet:
I can see the omen of coming trouble.

THESEUS

Alas, here is endless sorrow upon sorrow.
It passes speech, passes endurance.   875

CHORUS LEADER

What is it? Tell us if we may share the story.

THESEUS

It cries aloud, this tablet, cries aloud,
and Death is its song!
How shall I escape this weight of evils? I am ruined, destroyed.
What a song I have seen, sung in this writing!   880

CHORUS LEADER

Ah! Your speech shows a prelude of ruin!

THESEUS

I shall no longer hold this secret prisoner
in the gates of my mouth. It is horrible,
yet I will speak.
Citizens!
Hippolytus has dared to rape my wife.   885
He has dishonored Zeus's holy sunlight.
Father Poseidon, once you gave to me
three curses.... Now with one of these, I pray,
kill my son. Suffer him not to escape
this very day, if you have promised truly.   890

CHORUS LEADER

Call back your curses, King, call back your curses.
Else you will realize that you were wrong
another day, too late. I pray you, trust me.

THESEUS

I will not. And I now make this addition:
I banish him from this land's boundaries.
So fate shall strike him, one way or the other,
either Poseidon will respect my curse,   895
and send him dead into the house of Hades,
or exiled from this land, a beggar wandering,
on foreign soil, his life shall suck the dregs
of sorrow's cup.

CHORUS LEADER

Here comes your son, at the right moment, King Theseus.
Give over your deadly anger, you will best   900
determine for the welfare of your house.

(Enter Hippolytus with cosmpanions from the side.)

HIPPOLYTUS

I heard you crying, father, and came quickly.
I know no cause why you should mourn.
Tell me.

(He sees the body of Phaedra.)

O father, father—I see your wife! She's dead!   905
I cannot believe it. But a few moments since
I left her. . . . And just now she was still alive.
But what could it be? How did she die, father?
I must hear the truth from you. You say nothing to me?   910
When you are in trouble is no time for silence.
The heart that would hear everything
is proved most greedy in misfortune's hour.
You should not hide your troubles from your friends,
and, father, those who are closer than your friends.   915

THESEUS

What fools men are! You work and work for nothing,
you teach ten thousand skills to one another,
invent, discover everything. One thing only
you do not know: one thing you never hunted for—
a way to teach intelligence to fools.   920

HIPPOLYTUS

Clever indeed
would be the teacher able to compel
the stupid to be wise! But this is no time
for such fine logic chopping.
                          I am afraid
your tongue runs wild through sorrow.

THESEUS

                          If there were
some token now, some mark to make the division   925
clear between friend and friend, the true and the false!
All men should have two voices, one the just voice,
and one as chance would have it. In this way
the treacherous scheming voice would be confuted   930
by the just, and we should never be deceived.

HIPPOLYTUS

Has some friend poisoned your ear and slandered me?
Am I suspected despite my innocence?
I am amazed. I am amazed to hear
your words. They are distraught. They go indeed
far wide of the mark! 935

THESEUS

The mind of man—how far will it advance?
Where will its daring impudence find limits?
If human villainy and human life
shall grow in due proportion during a man's life,
if the one who's later shall always grow in wickedness
past the earlier, the gods must add another 940
world to this one, to hold all the villains.
    Look at this man! He is my son and he
dishonored my wife's bed! By the dead's testimony
he's clearly proved the vilest, falsest wretch. 945
Come—since you have already reached depravity—
show me your face; show it to me, your father.
    So you are the veritable holy man?
You walked with gods in purity immaculate?
I'll not believe your arrogant boasts: the gods 950
are not at all so stupid as you think.
Go, boast that you eat no meat, that you have Orpheus
for your king. Read until you are demented
your great thick books whose substance is as smoke.
For I have found you out. I tell you all, 955
avoid such men as he. They hunt their prey
with holy-seeming words, but their designs
are black and ugly. She is dead. You thought
that this would save you? Wretch, it is chiefly that
which proves your guilt. What oath that you can swear, 960
what speech that you can make for your acquittal,
outweighs her body here? You'll say, to be sure,

she was your enemy and that the bastard son
is always hateful to the legitimate line.
Your words would argue her a foolish merchant
whose stock of merchandise was her own life,
if she should throw away what she held dearest
to gratify her enmity for you.   965
    Or will you tell me that this frantic folly
is part of woman's nature but a man
is different? Yet I know that young men
are no more to be trusted than are women
when Cypris disturbs the youthful blood in them.
But the very male in them helps and protects them.   970
But why should I debate against you in words?
Here is the woman dead, the surest witness.
Get from this land with all the speed you can
to exile—may you rot there! Never again
come to our city, god-built Athens, nor
to any land over which my spear is king.   975
    If I should take this injury at your hands
and pardon you, then Sinis of the Isthmus,
whom once I killed, would vow I never killed him,
but only bragged of the deed. And Sciron's rocks
washed by the sea would call me liar when
I swore I was a terror to ill-doers.   980

CHORUS LEADER
    I cannot say of any man: he is happy.
    See here how former happiness lies uprooted!

HIPPOLYTUS
    Your furious spirit is terrifying, father:
    but this subject, though it's dressed in eloquence,
    if you will lay the matter bare of words,   985
    you'll find it is not eloquent. I am
    no man to speak with vapid, precious skill
    before a mob, although among my equals

and in a narrow circle I am held
not unaccomplished as a speaker.
That is as it should be. The demagogue
who charms a crowd is scorned by wiser judges.
But here in this necessity I must speak. 990
First I shall take the argument you first
urged as so irrefutable and deadly.
You see the earth and air about you, father?
In all of that there lives no man more pure
or temperate than I, though you deny it. 995

It is my rule to honor the gods first
and then to have as friends only such men
as try to do no wrong, men who feel shame
at ordering evil or treating others meanly
in return for kindness. I am no mocker
of my companions. Those who are my friends 1000
find me as much their friend when they are absent
as when we are together.

There is one thing that I have never done, the thing
of which you think that you convict me, father.
I am a virgin to this very day.
Save what I have heard or what I have seen in pictures, 1005
I'm ignorant of the deed. Nor do I wish
to see such things, for I've a maiden soul.
But say you disbelieve my temperance.
Then tell me how I came to be corrupted:
was it because she was more beautiful
than all the other women in the world? 1010
Or did I think that by taking her,
I'd win your place and kingdom for a dowry
and live in your own house? I would have been
a fool, a senseless fool, if I had dreamed it.
Was monarchy so sweet? Never, I tell you,
for the wise. A man whom power has so enchanted
must be demented. I would wish to be 1015

first in the athletic contests of the Greeks,
but in the city I'd take second place
and an enduring happy life among
the best society who are my friends.
So one can do what he wants, and danger's absence
has charms above the royal diadem.   1020
    But one word more and my defense is finished.
If I possessed a witness to my character,
if I were tried when she still saw the light,
deeds would have helped you as you scanned your friends
to know the true from the false. But now I swear,
I swear to you by Zeus, the god of oaths,   1025
by this deep-rooted fundament of earth,
I never did you wrong with your own wife
nor would have wished or even thought of it.
If I have been a villain, may I die
unfamed, unknown, a homeless stateless beggar,
an exile! May the earth and sea refuse   1030
to take my body in when I am dead!
    Out of what fear your wife took her own life
I do not know. More I may not say.
Pure she was in deed, although not pure:
I that have purity have used it to my ruin.   1035

CHORUS LEADER
    You have rebutted the charge enough by your oath:
    it is a great pledge you took in the gods' name.

THESEUS
    Why, here's a spell-binding magician for you!
    He wrongs his father and then trusts his craft,
    his smooth beguiling craft to lull my anger.   1040

HIPPOLYTUS
    Father, I must wonder at this in you.
    If I were your father now, and you my son,

I would not have banished you to exile! I
would have killed you if I thought you touched my wife.

THESEUS

This speech is worthy of you: but you'll not die so,   1045
by this rule that you have laid down for yourself.
A quick death is the easiest of ends
for a miserable man. No, you'll go wandering
far from your fatherland and beg your way
in foreign lands, draining dry a bitter life.
This is the payment of the impious man.°   1050

HIPPOLYTUS

What will you do? You will not wait until
time's pointing finger proves me innocent?
Must I then go at once to banishment?

THESEUS

Yes, and had I the power, your place of exile
would be beyond Pontus and Atlas' pillars.
That is the measure of my hate, my son.

HIPPOLYTUS

Pledges, oaths, and oracles—you will not test them?   1055
You will banish me from the kingdom without trial?

THESEUS

This letter here is proof without lot-casting.
As for the birds that fly above my head:
a long good-bye to them.

HIPPOLYTUS

                            Eternal gods!
Why don't I speak, since I am ruined now   1060
through loyalty to the oath I took by you?
No, he would not believe who should believe,
and I should be false to my oath for nothing.

THESEUS

Here's more of that holy and haughty manner of yours!
I cannot stomach it. Away with you!
Get from this country—and go quickly!   1065

HIPPOLYTUS

Where shall I turn? What friend will take me in,
when I am banished on a charge like this?

THESEUS

Doubtless some man who loves to entertain
a wife's seducer, a housemate in wickedness.

HIPPOLYTUS

That blow went home.   1070
I am near crying when I think that I
am judged to be wicked and that it is you who are judge.

THESEUS

You should have sobbed and thought of that before,
when you resolved to rape your father's wife.

HIPPOLYTUS

My house, if only you could speak for me!
Take voice and testify if I am wicked.   1075

THESEUS

You have a clever trick of citing witnesses
whose testimony is mute. Here is your handiwork.

(He points to the body.)

It, too, can't speak—but it convicts you.

HIPPOLYTUS

Ah!
If I could only find
another me to look me in the face
and see my tears and all that I am suffering!

THESEUS

Yes, in self-worship you are certainly practiced.   1080
You are more at home there than in the other virtues,
justice, for instance, and duty toward a father.

HIPPOLYTUS

Unhappy mother mine, and bitter birth pangs,
when you gave me to the world! I would not wish
on any of my friends a bastard's birth.

THESEUS   *(To the servants.)*

Drag him away!
Did you not hear me, men, a long time since
proclaiming his decree of banishment?   1085

HIPPOLYTUS

Let one of them touch me at his peril! But you,
you drive me out yourself—if you have the heart!

THESEUS

I'll do it, too, unless you obey my orders.
No pity for your exile will change my heart.

(Exit Theseus into the house.)

HIPPOLYTUS

So, I'm condemned and there is no escape.   1090
I know the truth but cannot tell the truth.

(To the statue of Artemis.)

Daughter of Leto, dearest of the gods to me,
comrade and partner in the hunt, behold me,
banished from famous Athens.
Farewell, city! Farewell, Erechtheus' land!   1095
Troezen, farewell! So many happy times
you knew to give a young man, growing up.
This is the last time I shall look upon you,
the last time I shall greet you.

(To his companions.)

Come friends, you are of my age and of this country,
say your farewells and set me on my way.
You'll never see a man more pure and temperate—   1100
even if my father thinks that I am not.

(Exit Hippolytus to the side.)

CHORUS OF HUNTSMEN° [*singing*]
                    STROPHE A
The care of the gods for us is a great thing,
whenever it comes to my mind:
it plucks the burden of sorrow from me.
So I have a secret hope of knowledge;   1105
but my hopes grow dim when I see
the deeds of men and their destinies.
For fortune is ever veering, and the currents of men's lives are
    shifting,
wandering forever.   1110

CHORUS OF WOMEN [*singing*]
                    ANTISTROPHE A
This is the lot in life I seek
and I pray that the gods may grant it me,
luck and prosperity
and a heart untroubled by anguish;
and a mind that is neither inflexible
nor false clipped coin,   1115
that I may easily change my ways,
my ways of today when tomorrow comes,
and so be happy all my life long.

CHORUS OF HUNTSMEN°
                    STROPHE B
My heart is no longer clear: 1120
I have seen what I never dreamed.

I have seen the brightest star of Athens,°
stricken by a father's wrath,
banished to an alien land. 1125
Sands of the seashore!
Thicket of the mountain!
Where with his pacing hounds
he hunted wild beasts and killed
to the honor of holy Dictynna. 1130

CHORUS OF WOMEN

ANTISTROPHE B

He will never again mount his car
with its span of Venetian mares,
nor fill the ring of Limnae with the sound of horses' hoofs.
The music that never slept
on the strings of his lyre, shall be mute, 1135
shall be mute in his father's house.
The haunts of the maiden goddess
in the deep, rich meadow shall lack their crowns.
You are banished: there's an end 1140
of the rivalry of maids for your love.

EPODE

But my sorrow shall not die;
still my eyes shall be wet with tears
for your dreadful doom.
Sad mother, you bore him in vain; 1145
I am angry against the gods.
Sister Graces, why did you let him go,
guiltless, out of his native land,
out of his father's house? 1150

CHORUS LEADER

But here I see Hippolytus' servant,
in haste making for the house, his face sorrowful.

(Enter a Messenger° from the side.)

MESSENGER

Where shall I go to find King Theseus, women?
If you know, tell me. Is he within doors?   1155

CHORUS

Here he is coming out.

MESSENGER

Theseus, I bring you news worthy of distress
for you and all the citizens who live
in Athens' walls and boundaries of Troezen.

THESEUS

What is it? Has some still newer disaster   1160
seized my two neighboring cities?

MESSENGER

Hippolytus is dead: I may almost say dead:
he sees the light of day still, though the balance
that holds him in this world is slight indeed.

THESEUS

Who killed him? I can guess that someone hated him,
whose wife he raped, as he did mine, his father's.   1165

MESSENGER

It was the horses of his own car that killed him,
they, and the curses of your lips,
the curses you invoked against your son,
and prayed the lord of ocean to fulfill them.

THESEUS

O gods—Poseidon, you are then truly
my father! You have heard my prayers!   1170
How did he die? Tell me. How did the beam
of Justice's deadfall strike him, my dishonorer?

MESSENGER

We were combing our horses' coats beside the sea,

where the waves came crashing to the shore. And we were
    crying,
for one had come and told us that our master,   1175
Hippolytus, should walk this land no more,
since you had laid hard banishment upon him.
Then he came himself down to the shore to us,
with the same refrain of tears,
and with him walked a countless company
of friends and young men his own age.   1180
    But at last he gave over crying and said:
"Why do I rave like this? It is my father
who has commanded and I must obey him.
Prepare my horses, men, and harness them.
For this no longer is a city of mine."
Then every man made haste. Before you could say the words,   1185
we had made the horses ready before our master.
He put his feet into the driver's rings,
and took the reins from the rail into his hands.
But first he folded his hands and prayed the gods: 1190
"Zeus, let me die now, if I have been wicked!
Let my father perceive that he has done me wrong,
whether I live to see the day or not."
    With that, he took the goad and touched the horses.
And we his servants followed our master's car,   1195
close by the horses' heads, on the straight road
that leads to Argos and to Epidaurus.
When we were entering the lonely country
the other side of the border, where the shore   1200
goes down to the Saronic Gulf, a rumbling
deep down in the earth, terrible to hear,
roared loudly like the thunder of Father Zeus.
The horses raised their heads, pricked up their ears,
and mighty fear was on us all to know
whence came the sound. As we looked toward the shore,   1205
where the waves were beating, we saw a wave appear,

a miracle wave, lifting its crest to the sky,
so high that Sciron's coast was blotted out
from my eye's vision. And it hid the Isthmus
and the Asclepius Rock. To the shore it came,   1210
swelling, boiling, crashing, casting its surf around,
to where the chariot stood.
But at the very moment when it broke,
the wave threw up a monstrous savage bull.
Its bellowing filled the land, and the land echoed it,   1215
with shuddering emphasis. And for those who saw it
the sight was too great to bear. Then sudden panic
fell on the horses in the car. But the master—
he was used to horses' ways—all his life long
he had been with horses—took firm grip of the reins   1220
and lashed the ends behind his back and pulled
like a sailor at the oar. The horses bolted:
their teeth were clenched upon the fire-forged bit.
They heeded neither the driver's hand nor harness
nor the jointed car. As often as he would turn them   1225
with guiding hand to the soft sand of the shore,
the bull appeared in front to head them off,
maddening the team with terror.
But when in frenzy they charged toward the cliffs,   1230
the bull came galloping beside the rail,
silently following—until he brought disaster,
capsizing the car, striking the wheel on a rock.
Then all was in confusion. The naves of wheels
and axle pins flew up into the air,   1235
and he the unlucky driver, tangled in the reins,
was dragged along in an inextricable
knot, and his dear head pounded on the rocks,
his body bruised. He cried aloud and terrible
his voice rang in our ears: "Stand, horses, stand!   1240
You were fed in my stables. Do not kill me!
My father's curse! His curse! Will none of you
save me? I am a good, true man. Save me!"

Many of us had will enough, but all
were left behind. Cut somehow free of the reins,
he fell. There was still a little life in him.   1245
But the horses vanished and that ill-omened monster,
somewhere, I know not where, in the rough cliffs.

I am only a slave in your household, your majesty,
but I shall never be able to believe   1250
that your son was wicked, not though the race of women
were all hanged for it, not though they filled with writing
the whole of the pine forest on Mount Ida—
for I know that he's a good and noble man.

CHORUS LEADER

It has been fulfilled, this bitter, new disaster: 1255
from what is doomed and fated there's no escape.

THESEUS

For hatred of the sufferer I was glad
at what you told me. Still, he was my son.
As such I have reverence for him and for the gods:
I neither rejoice nor sorrow at these evils.   1260

MESSENGER

What is your pleasure that we do with him?
Would you have him brought to you? If I might counsel,
do not be harsh with your son—now that he's ruined.

THESEUS

Bring him to me that I may see his face.   1265
He swore that he had never wronged my bed.
I'll refute him with the gods' own punishing stroke.

(Exit Messenger to the side.)

CHORUS [singing]
Cypris, you guide the inflexible hearts of gods
and of men,
and with you
comes Eros with the flashing wings,   1270

with the swiftest of wings.
Over the earth he flies
and the loud-echoing salt sea.
Winged, golden, he bewitches and maddens the heart
of the victim he swoops upon.   1275
He bewitches the whelps of the mountains
and of the sea,
and all the creatures that earth feeds,
and the blazing sun sees—
and men, too—
over all you hold royal dominion,   1280
Cypris, you are only ruler
over all these.

                    (Artemis appears on the roof of the house.)

ARTEMIS [chanting]
I call on you, noble son of Aegeus,
to hear me! It is I,
Artemis, child of Leto.   1285
     Theseus, poor man, what joy have you here?
You have murdered your son most impiously.
Dark indeed was the conclusion
you drew from your wife's lying stories,
but plain to see is the destruction
to which they led you.
There's a hell underground: haste to it,   1290
and hide your head there! Or will you take wings,
choose the life of a bird instead of a man,
keep your feet from treading destruction's path?
Among good men, at least, you have no share in life.   1295

[speaking]

     Hear, Theseus, how these evils came to pass.
I shall gain nothing, but I'll give you pain.
I've come for this—to show that your son's heart
was always just, so that in his death

his good name may live on. I will show you, too,
the frenzied love that seized your wife, or I may call it   1300
a noble innocence. For that most hated goddess,
hated by all of us whose joy is virginity,
drove her with love's sharp prickings to desire
your son. She tried her best to vanquish Cypris
with the mind's power, but at last against her will
she was destroyed by the nurse's stratagems,   1305
who told your son under oath her mistress loved him.
But he, just man, did not fall in with her
counsels, and even when reviled by you
refused to break the oath that he had pledged.
Such was his piety. But your wife feared
lest she be put to the proof and wrote a letter,   1310
a letter full of lies; and so she killed
your son by treachery; but she convinced you.

THESEUS
   Alas!

ARTEMIS

[handwritten: shows up at the end and tells the truth]

   This is a bitter story, Theseus. Stay,
hear further, that you may sorrow all the more.
You know you had three curses from your father,   1315
three, clear for you to use? One you have launched,
vile wretch, at your own son, when you might have
spent it upon an enemy. Your father,
king of the sea, in loving kindness to you
gave you, as he had promised, all he ought.
But you've been proven wicked both in his eyes   1320
and mine in that you did not stay for oaths
nor voice of oracles, nor put to proof,
nor let long time investigate—too quickly
you hurled the curses at your son and killed him.

THESEUS
   Mistress, I am destroyed.

ARTEMIS

What you have done indeed is dreadful—but   1325
you still might gain forgiveness for these things.
For it was Cypris managed the thing this way
to gratify her anger against Hippolytus.
This is the settled custom of the gods:
No one may fly in the face of another's wish:
we remain aloof and neutral. Else, I assure you,   1330
had I not feared Zeus, I never would have endured
such shame as this—my best friend among men
killed, and I could do nothing.
As for you, in the first place ignorance acquits you,
and then your wife, by dying, destroyed the chance   1335
to test her words, and thus convinced your mind.
You, Theseus, are the one who suffers most—
misfortune for you, but also grief for me.
The gods do not rejoice when the pious die;   1340
the wicked we destroy, children, house and all.

(Enter Hippolytus from the side, supported by attendants.)

CHORUS [chanting]
Here comes the suffering Hippolytus,
his fair young body and his golden head
a battered wreck. O trouble of the house,
what double sorrow from the hand of a god   1345
has been fulfilled for this our royal palace!

HIPPOLYTUS [chanting]
A battered wreck of body! Unjust father,
and oracle unjust—this is your work.
Woe for my fate!   1350
My head is filled with shooting agony,
and in my brain there is a leaping fire.
Let me be!
For I would rest my weary frame awhile.
Ah, ah!

Curse on my team! How often have I fed you 1355
from my own hand—you've killed, you've murdered me!
Oh, oh!
By the gods, gently! Servants, lay hands
lightly on my wounded body.
Who is this standing on the right of me? 1360
Come lift me carefully, bear me easily,
a man unlucky, by my own father cursed
in bitter error. Zeus, do you see this,
see me that worshipped the gods in piety, 1365
me that outdid all men in purity,
see me now go to death that gapes before me;
all my life lost, and all for nothing,
labors of piety in the face of men?

[singing]

Ah, ah!
Oh, the pain, the pain that comes upon me! 1370
Let me be, let me be, wretched as I am!
May death the healer come for me at last!
You kill me ten times over with this pain.
O for a spear with a keen cutting edge 1375
to shear me apart—and give me my last sleep!
Father, your deadly curse!
This evil comes from some manslaying of old, 1380
some ancient tale of murder among kin.
But why should it strike me, who am clear of guilt?
Alas!
What is there to say? How can I painlessly shake 1385
from my life this agony? O death, black night of death,
resistless death, come to me now the miserable,
and give me sleep!

ARTEMIS

Unhappy boy! You are yoked to a cruel fate.
The nobility of your mind has proved your ruin. 1390

HIPPOLYTUS [*now speaking*]

Wait!
O divine fragrance! Even in my pain
I sense it, and the suffering is lightened.
The goddess Artemis is in this place.

ARTEMIS

She is, poor man, the dearest god to you.

HIPPOLYTUS

You see my suffering, mistress?   1395

ARTEMIS

I see it. But the law forbids my tears.

HIPPOLYTUS

Gone is your huntsman, gone your servant now.

ARTEMIS

Yes, truly: but you die beloved by me.

HIPPOLYTUS

Gone is your groom, gone your shrine's guardian.

ARTEMIS

Cypris, the worker of mischief, so contrived.   1400

HIPPOLYTUS

Alas, I know now the goddess who destroyed me!

ARTEMIS

She blamed your disrespect, hated your temperance.

HIPPOLYTUS

She is but one—yet ruined all three of us.

ARTEMIS

Yes, you, your father, and his wife, all three.

HIPPOLYTUS

Indeed I'm sorry for my father's suffering.   1405

ARTEMIS

He was deceived by a goddess' cunning snares.

HIPPOLYTUS

O father, this is great sorrow for you!

THESEUS

I am done for; I have no joy left in life.

HIPPOLYTUS

I sorrow for you in this more than for me.

THESEUS

Would that it was I who was dying instead of you!   1410

HIPPOLYTUS

How bitter your father Poseidon's gifts, how bitter!

THESEUS

Would that they had never come into my mouth.

HIPPOLYTUS

Even without them, you would still have killed me—
you were so angry.

THESEUS

                    Gods tripped up my judgment.

HIPPOLYTUS

O, if only men might be a curse to gods!   1415

ARTEMIS

Enough! Though dead, you'll not be unavenged,
Cypris shall find the angry shafts she hurled
against you shall cost her dear, and this will be
your recompense for piety and goodness.   1420
Another mortal, whichever one she loves
the most, I'll punish with these unerring arrows
shot from my own hand.
    To you, unfortunate Hippolytus,
by way of compensation for these ills,

I will give the greatest honors of Troezen.
Unwedded maids before the day of marriage   1425
will cut their hair in your honor. You will reap
through the long cycle of time a rich reward in tears.
And when young girls sing songs, they will not forget you,
your name will not be left unmentioned,
nor Phaedra's love for you remain unsung.   1430

(To Theseus.)

Son of old Aegeus, take your son
to your embrace. Draw him to you. Unknowing
you killed him. It is natural for men
to err when they are blinded by the gods.

(To Hippolytus.)

And you, don't bear a grudge against your father.   1435
It was your fate that you should die this way.
Farewell, I must not look upon the dead.
My eye must not be polluted by the last
gaspings for breath. I see you are near this.

HIPPOLYTUS   *(Exit Artemis.)*
Farewell to you, too, holy maiden! Go in peace.   1440
You lightly leave a long companionship.
You bid me end my quarrel with my father,
and I obey. In the past, too, I obeyed you.
Ah!
The darkness is upon my eyes already.
Father, lay hold on me and lift me up.   1445

THESEUS
Alas, what are you doing to me, my son?

HIPPOLYTUS
I am dying. I can see the gates of death.

THESEUS
And so you leave me, my hands stained with murder.

HIPPOLYTUS

No, for I free you from all guilt in this.

THESEUS

You will acquit me of blood guiltiness?   1450

HIPPOLYTUS

So help me Artemis of the conquering bow!

THESEUS

Dear son, how noble you have proved to me!

HIPPOLYTUS

Farewell to you, too, father, a long farewell!   1455

THESEUS

Alas for your goodness and your piety.

HIPPOLYTUS

Yes, pray that your trueborn sons will prove as good!

THESEUS

Dear son, bear up. Do not forsake me.

HIPPOLYTUS

This is the end of what I have to bear.
I'm gone, father. Cover my face up quickly.

THESEUS

Pallas Athena's famous city,
what a man you will have lost! Alas for me!   1460
Cypris, your evils I shall long remember.

CHORUS [*chanting*]

This common grief for all the city,°
it came unlooked for. A constant stream
of manifold tears will beat down on us;
for lamentable stories about the great   1465
affect us all the more.

                                        (*Exit all.*)

TEXTUAL NOTES

(The line numbers indicated are in some cases only approximate.)

ALCESTIS

Characters: The list of characters prefixed to the play in the manuscripts identifies the boy's name as Eumelus, but there is nothing to support this in the play itself and it is probably just an ancient scholarly guess. In Homer's *Iliad* Eumelus is the son of Admetus and Alcestis.

16: Many scholars reject this line as an interpolation.

77: The manuscripts indicate that different members of the chorus chant or sing the various sections of the following entrance song; editors differ on the exact distribution.

93–94: Text uncertain.

207–8: These two lines are identical to *Hecuba* 411-12 and are probably an interpolation here.

211: Many editors divide the chorus here into groups and distribute the various sections of this song to different groups.

215: Text uncertain.

312: The manuscripts add here the line, "He can talk with him and be spoken to in turn." This is rejected by most scholars as an interpolation (cf. 195).

393: See note on Characters above.

411: About a line of text is missing here.

458: This line is rejected by some scholars; if it is retained, then a line must be missing before 469 (in the antistrophe).

469: See on line 458 (in the strophe).

603: The manuscripts are punctuated to read, "*All of wisdom is there in the noble. I stand in awe, and good hope . . .*" The translation reflects a modern repunctuation.

651–52: These two lines are almost identical to 295–96 and are rejected here by most scholars as an interpolation.

708: Some manuscripts read not "have spoken" but "am speaking."

795–96: The words "put flowers on your head" and "fight down these present troubles" are repeated in the Greek text in lines 829 and 832, and are probably an interpolation here.

818–19: These two lines are said by ancient commentators to have been missing in some manuscripts, and are rejected by most modern scholars.

MEDEA

12: Text uncertain.

36: This line is rejected by some scholars as an interpolation.

40–43: Some or all of these lines are rejected by most scholars as interpolations.

87: This line is probably an interpolation.

223–24: These lines are rejected by some scholars as an interpolation.

246: This line is rejected by many scholars as an interpolation.

262: Rejected by many scholars as an interpolation.

304: This line is probably an interpolation.

355–56: Some scholars reject these lines as an interpolation.

357: This line is placed by some scholars after the following one and is rejected by other scholars as an interpolation.

468: This line is probably an interpolation.

626: Text uncertain.

725–29: The order of these lines is uncertain, and some or all of them are rejected by many scholars as an interpolation.

778–79: The first of these two lines, or both of them, are rejected by some scholars as an interpolation.

782: This line is probably an interpolation.

785: Probably an interpolation.

798-99: These lines are rejected by many scholars as an interpolation.

856-57: Text uncertain.

910: Text uncertain.

928: This line is rejected by some scholars as an interpolation.

949: Probably an interpolation.

1006-7: These lines are probably an interpolation.

1056-80: Some or all of these lines are rejected by some scholars as an interpolation.

1121: Rejected by most scholars as an interpolation.

1220-21: Some scholars reject the second of these two lines, or both of them, as an interpolation; in addition, the text of the second one is uncertain.

1233-35: These lines are rejected by most scholars as an interpolation.

1273-74: The order and location of these lines are uncertain.

1316: Rejected by some scholars as an interpolation.

1359: Rejected by some scholars as an interpolation.

1388: Rejected by some scholars as an interpolation.

1415-19: These lines are rejected by most scholars as an interpolation.

CHILDREN OF HERACLES

75: Perhaps some words are missing.

102: Text uncertain.

110: After this line some lines are probably missing.

149: Text uncertain.

169: Text uncertain.

184: This is a widely accepted scholarly emendation for "nothing in turn," the reading found in the manuscripts.

217: Some editors think that a few lines are missing after this.

219: Or "from the impregnable recesses of Hades."

236: The manuscripts have "path of conscience."

237: The manuscripts have "reject these visitors."

299-301: These three lines are in the manuscripts, but are rejected by most editors.

312: A line may be missing after this.

345: Or possibly, "We will remain here and pray ..."

396: The reading is uncertain; "formation" is a conjecture.

402: This line, "to ensure ... for the city," is deleted or moved (e.g., to after 409) by some editors.

405: This line is deleted by many editors.

486: Text uncertain: possibly "Our course, which ..."

505: The translation reflects the manuscript reading. Some editors emend to, "when we could save them."

529: Reading uncertain.

582: Text uncertain: perhaps "the things my own heart will fail to get."

592: Or possibly, "This, instead of children, is the treasure of my maiden-hood."

613: Possibly "one house."

614: Text uncertain.

640: Text uncertain.

683: The correct order of lines 683-90 is disputed.

689: Or possibly "they'll be fighting."

785: Text uncertain.

788: Text uncertain.

793: Text uncertain.

805-6: A line or more seems to be missing after 805; I have supplied the necessary sense.

822: Text uncertain.

838: Text uncertain.

884: Text uncertain: "grovel" is a conjecture; possibly "see him alive."

949: The order of lines in 947-52 is disputed.

970: Some lines may be missing after this.

1014-15: Text and interpretation uncertain: in particular, *prostropaion* may mean "hallowed," or "suppliant," or "vengeance-seeking," or "pollution-causing."

1038: Reading uncertain.

1040-41: Or possibly: "Never let libations and blood offerings / cease flowing from your hands onto my tomb."

1047: Some editors delete this line and the reference to "kill" in the previous line.

1051: Some editors excise this phrase, which appears to contradict the oracle about a hero's tomb for Eurystheus' body; others suggest that lines have fallen out immediately after this, in which Alcmene's command is countermanded.

1053: Many scholars believe some lines are lost here, before the final words of the chorus.

HIPPOLYTUS

Characters: See textual note on line 1153.

101: An ancient papyrus reads not "before your gates, the goddess Cypris," but rather "before your gates, nearby."

103-8: The translation follows the order of these lines in the manuscripts; many editors have proposed various transpositions of them.

191-97: These lines are suspected by some scholars of being an interpolation.

601: Scholars disagree about the staging of the following scene and especially about exactly where Phaedra is during the following interchange between Hippolytus and the Nurse—they take no notice of her, but she evidently hears most or all of what they say.

626: Text uncertain. Some scholars excise lines 626-27 as an interpolation.

634-37: These lines are suspected by some scholars of being an interpolation.

663: This line is suspected by many scholars of being an interpolation.

668-79: Most medieval manuscripts assign the following short song (the antistrophe to the strophe in lines 361-72) to the Nurse, but most modern scholars prefer, as do a few manuscripts, to give it to Phaedra.

680-81: The manuscripts assign these lines to the Chorus Leader, but it is probably better to give them to the Nurse.

844: A few words are missing here.

867-68: In the manuscripts there follow two lines of which the text and meaning are quite uncertain.

871-73: The ancient commentators report that these lines were missing in some manuscripts; they are rejected by many modern scholars as an interpolation.

1050: Ancient commentators report that this line was missing in many manuscripts; it is rejected by most modern scholars as an interpolation.

1102-50: In this ode, the chorus refers to itself with the masculine gender in the first strophe and with the feminine in the first antistrophe. Scholars disagree about whom to assign the ode to: the chorus of women (to whom the manuscripts attribute it), Hippolytus' hunting companions, or both in alternation (as we have printed it here).

1123: Text uncertain.

1153: This messenger may be identical with the old servant who spoke with Hippolytus at lines 88-120.

1462-66: Some scholars suspect these final lines of being due to a later author.

GLOSSARY

Acamas: son of Theseus; brother of Demophon; a legendary king of Athens.

Acastus: son of Pelias (the king of Iolcus); brother of Alcestis.

Achaea: a region in Greece on the northern coast of the Peloponnese; sometimes used to refer to all of Greece.

Acheron: one of the rivers of the underworld.

Admetus: son of Pheres; king of Pherae; husband of Alcestis.

Adriatic: the sea to the west of Greece between it and Italy.

Aegean: the sea to the east and south of Greece.

Aegeus: father of Theseus; king of Athens.

Aethra: daughter of Pittheus and mother of Theseus.

Alcathous: a legendary king of Megara, a city on the southern border of Attica.

Alcestis: daughter of Pelias (the king of Iolcus); wife of Admetus.

Alcmene: mother of Heracles.

Alpheus: a river in the Peloponnese in southern Greece; it flows along Olympia, the site of an important Greek religious center.

Amazons: a mythical race of warrior women who fought against the Athenians; one of them was said to have been the mother of Hippolytus by Theseus.

Ammon: an important Egyptian god, worshipped there and in neighboring countries at various temples with which oracles were associated.

Aphrodite: goddess of sexual desire.

Apollo: son of Zeus and Leto; twin brother of Artemis; god of prophecy, healing, archery, and poetry; his prophetic seat was at Delphi.

Ares: god of war.

Argo: the boat on which Jason and his crew, the Argonauts (including Admetus) sailed on their quest to obtain the Golden Fleece.

Argos: a city and region in the eastern Peloponnese in southern Greece, not always distinguished clearly from Mycenae.

Artemis: daughter of Zeus and Leto; twin sister of Apollo; goddess of the hunt, childbirth, and virginity, who protected wild animals and boys and girls before they reached adolescence; sometimes identified with Hecate.

Asclepius: son of Apollo; a legendary human or divine doctor capable of restoring the dead to life again.

Asclepius Rock: an unknown coastal feature, presumably near Epidaurus (where Asclepius was especially worshipped).

Athena: daughter of Zeus and Metis; goddess of wisdom and warfare; patron goddess of Athens.

Athens, Athenians: an important city (and its people) in the region of Attica in the east-central part of Greece; home of Greek tragedy.

Atlas: a mythical giant said to stand at the far western extremity of the world and to bear the heavens on his shoulders.

Atlas' Pillars: columns in the far west that were said to support the heavens; also called the Pillars of Heracles.

Attica: a region of east-central Greece dominated by and belonging to Athens.

Bacchant: an ecstatic female worshipper of Dionysus.

Bistones: a wild people who lived in Thrace.

Black Sea's lock: *see* Bosphorus' straits

Boebias: a small lake in southern Thessaly in north-central Greece, to the east of Pherae.

Bosphorus' straits: the channel connecting the Black Sea to the Sea of Marmara, which in turn is connected to the Aegean Sea by the Dardanelles.

Carneian: a month in the Spartan calendar (approximately August) during which the Carneian festival was celebrated in honor of Apollo.

Cecrops: a mythical king of Athens.

Cephalus: a hero of Athenian legend; the Dawn fell in love with him and carried him off to heaven.

Cephisus: a major river that waters the plain west of Athens.

Cerberus: the three-headed dog that guarded the underworld; one of Heracles' labors was to bring him up to the light.

Chalybes: a tribe near the Black Sea that was credited with the discovery of ironworking.

Charon: the ferryman who brought the souls of the dead across the water to the underworld.

Clashing Rocks: the two rocks (*Symplegades*), located at either side of the Bosphorus, that were said to crash together at random and crush ships as they passed through.

Colchis, Colchians: a region (and its people) located at the eastern end of the Black Sea (modern-day Georgia) around the mouth of the Phasis River (modern-day Rioni River).

Corinth: a large city in Greece on the isthmus connecting the Peloponnesus to central Greece.

Corybants: ecstatic dancers who worshipped the Phrygian goddess Cybele (the Great Mother).

Creon: a king of Corinth.

Crete: an important Greek island in the southeastern Mediterranean.

Cyclopes: divine ironworkers who forged Zeus' thunderbolts.

Cycnus: son of Ares; murderer of travelers until Heracles killed him.

Cypris: Aphrodite; according to some accounts she was born in the Mediterranean Sea near Cyprus and came first to land on that island, and she was worshipped in an especially strong cult there.

Demeter: goddess of fertility and crops; mother of Persephone.

Demophon: son of Theseus; brother of Acamas; a legendary king of Athens.

Dictynna: a Cretan mountain nymph identified with Artemis.

Diomedes: a giant of Thrace who ruled the Bistones and owned man-eating horses.

Dionysus: son of Zeus and Semele; god of wine, music, and theater; also known as Bacchus.

Dirce: a fountain and river in Thebes.

Electryon: son of Perseus and Andromeda; king of Tiryns; father of Alcmene.

Epidaurus: a small town in southeast Greece across the Saronic Gulf from Athens.

Erechtheus: a legendary king of Athens.

Eridanus: a mythological river thought vaguely to be situated somewhere in northern Europe.

Eros: son of Aphrodite; god of sexual desire.

Etruscan: name (in Greek: Tyrrhenian) used generically for the non-Greek inhabitants of Italy; famous for military trumpets.

Euboea: a large island off the coast of eastern mainland Greece, north of Athens.

Eurystheus: son of Sthenelus; legendary king of Tiryns or Argos; he imposed the twelve labors on Heracles.

Eurytus: king of Oechalia and father of Iole; defeated by Heracles.

Four Towns: an ancient confederation of four towns in Marathon which was said to have existed before Theseus unified Attica.

Girdle: in one of the exploits of Theseus and Heracles, they sought to obtain the girdle belonging to Hippolyta, queen of the Amazons.

Golden Fleece: the fleece of the winged ram that saved Phrixus and Helle, the children of Athamas and Nephele, from being sacrificed by their stepmother Ino.

Gorgon: one of three monstrous snake-women killed by Perseus.

Graces: companions of Aphrodite, goddesses of all kinds of beauty and charm.

Hades: brother of Zeus and Poseidon; god of the underworld; his name is used synonymously for the underworld itself.

Harmony: daughter of Aphrodite and Ares (or Hephaestus).

Hebe: the goddess of youth, married to Heracles after his death.

Hecate: goddess associated with witchcraft, night, doorways, crossroads, and the moon; sometimes identified with Artemis.

Helios: the sun; father of Aeëtes; grandfather of Medea.

Hellas: Greece.

Hera: wife and sister of Zeus; queen of the gods.

Heracles: son of Zeus and Alcmene; the greatest hero of Greek legend, famous for his physical strength and for his wildness in drinking and sexuality.

Hermes: son of Zeus and Maia; the messenger god; god of travelers, contests, stealth, and heralds, who accompanied the souls of the dead to the underworld.

Hesperian: western.

Hestia: the god of the hearth, honored in a shrine in the house.

Hippolytus: son of Theseus and an Amazon; object of a cult in Troezen in which girls about to be married dedicated a lock of their hair to him.

Hyllus: son of Heracles.

Hymenaeus: god of marriage.

Ino: stepmother of Phrixus and Helle (*see* Golden Fleece).

Iolaus: a nephew and comrade of Heracles who assisted him in many of his exploits as his charioteer.

Iolcus: a city in the southeastern region of Thessaly (modern-day Volos) in north-central Greece; Jason's hometown; the expedition for the Golden Fleece began from here.

Isthmus: the narrow strip of land connecting the Peloponnese in southern Greece to the rest of mainland Greece.

Jason: son of Aeson; husband of Medea; captain of the *Argo*.

Larisa: a city in Thessaly (north-central Greece).

Leto: goddess, the mother of Apollo and Artemis.

Libya: a region on the north coast of Africa.

Limnae: one of the five villages of the district of Laconia in the Peloponnese in southern Greece that went to make up Sparta; an important center of the worship of Artemis in the Peloponnese.

Lord of Ocean: Poseidon.

Loxias: Apollo.

Lycaon: son of Ares, killed by Heracles.

Lycia: a region in southwest Anatolia (modern Turkey).

Lydia: a region in west-central Anatolia (modern Turkey).

Marathon: an ancient Greek city in Attica near Athens.

Medea: daughter of Aeëtes, the king of Colchis; granddaughter of Helios; wife of Jason.

Mighty Mother: the Phrygian goddess Cybele, sometimes identified by the Greeks with Rhea, the Mother of the Gods.

Munychia: a hill in the port city of Piraeus near Athens.

Muses: daughters of Mnemosyne and Zeus, associated with all forms of cultural, especially artistic, excellence.

Mycenae: an ancient city in Greece in the northeastern Peloponnese, not always distinguished clearly from nearby Argos.

Naiad: a nymph associated with fountains and streams.

Oechalian: from Oechalia, an ancient legendary city of unknown location captured famously by Heracles.

Olympus: a mountain on which the gods make their home, located in Pieria in northern Greece.

Orpheus: son of Apollo and Calliope (one of the Muses); one of the Argonauts; a legendary poet whose enchanting music had the power to move animals, trees, and even rocks, and was almost able to bring back his beloved Eurydice from the dead.

Othrys: a mountain in central Greece.

Paean: a name for Apollo as a healer and savior.

Pallantids: the fifty children of the legendary Athenian hero Pallas, nobles who fought against Theseus and were killed by him.

Pallas: Athena.

Pallene: a small town in Attica, east of Athens.

Pan: a rustic, musical god dwelling in wild nature and associated with sudden mental disturbances (hence our term "panic").

Pandion: a legendary king of Athens.

Peirene: a nymph whose son with Poseidon, Cenchrias, was accidentally killed by Artemis; she became a spring outside Corinth.

Pelasgian: Greek, and especially Argive, from a word denoting the earliest inhabitants of part or all of what is now Greece.

Pelian: from Pelion, a mountain in the southeastern part of Thessaly (north-central Greece).

Pelias: father of Alcestis; half-brother of Aeson, Jason's father, from whom Pelias stole the throne of Iolcus. Jason makes his quest for the Golden

Fleece because Pelias has promised to return the throne to him if he is able to retrieve it.

Pelion: a mountain located in the southeastern region of Thessaly (north-central Greece) that towers over Iolcus.

Pelops: a mythical king of the city of Pisa in the Peloponnese in southern Greece; father of Pittheus.

Persephone: daughter of Demeter; queen of the underworld.

Perseus: legendary hero who killed the Gorgon Medusa.

Phaethon: a son of Apollo who was killed when he tried to drive his father's chariot of the sun and was mourned by his sisters.

Pherae: town in southeastern Thessaly in north-central Greece.

Pheres: king of Pherae; father of Admetus.

Phoebus: epithet of Apollo meaning "bright."

Phrygian: from Phrygia, a region in west-central Anatolia (modern Turkey).

Pierian nine: the Muses.

Pittheus: a king of Troezen; son of Pelops; father of Theseus; regarded as one of the wise men of antiquity.

Pontus: the Black Sea.

Pythian: referring to Apollo, from Delphi (where Apollo had killed the monstrous Python), his major oracle and cult center, situated on Mount Parnassus in central Greece.

Salty Lake: a coastal lagoon to the north of Troezen, separated from the Saronic Gulf by a long sandbar.

Saronic Gulf: a body of water to the southwest of Athens, bounded on the northeast by Attica, on the northwest by the Isthmus of Corinth, and on the southwest by the Peloponnese.

Sciron: a mythical brigand who pushed travelers over a cliff to their death; Theseus punished and killed him in the same way.

Scylla: a six-headed female monster who lived in a cave opposite Charybdis, a giant whirlpool, in the Strait of Messina and fed on passing sailors.

Semele: a Theban princess, mother of Dionysus by Zeus.

Sinis: a mythical bandit who killed travelers by tying them between two bent pine trees and then cutting the trees free; Theseus punished and killed him in the same way.

Sisypheans: the people of Corinth, named from its legendary founder Sisyphus.

Sisyphus: legendary founder of Corinth; a trickster figure who famously deceived the gods on multiple occasions.

Sparta: an important Greek town in the Peloponnese in southern Greece.

Sthenelus: father of Eurystheus, king of Tiryns.

Thebes: a large city in the southern part of the region of Boeotia in central Greece.

Themis: primeval goddess of custom and established law.

Theseus: son of Aegeus and Aethra; the most important hero of Athenian legend.

Thessaly: a large region in the north-central part of Greece.

Thrace: a wild region to the northeast of Greece (modern Balkans).

Tiryns: ancient Greek city in the southeastern Peloponnese.

Trachis: a region and city in central Greece.

Tro(e)zen: a small town in the northeastern Peloponnese in southern Greece near the southwest coast of the Saronic Gulf, facing Attica.

Tyrrhenian Sea: the body of water limited by Sardinia to the west, Italy to the east, and Sicily to the south. Its southeastern extremity is the Strait of Messina, where Scylla and Charybdis were thought to be located.

Venetian: from an area to the northwest of the Adriatic Sea famous for its horses.

Zeus: king of gods and men; father of Heracles and many other gods and heroes.